The
American
Revolution:

RESS. JULY 4, 1776.

of the thirteen united States of Amer

Whose
Revolution?

# THE
# AMERICAN REVOLUTION:
# WHOSE REVOLUTION?

edited by
## JAMES KIRBY MARTIN
and
## KAREN R. STUBAUS

ROBERT E. KRIEGER PUBLISHING COMPANY
Huntington, New York
1977

Original edition 1977

Printed and Published by
ROBERT E. KRIEGER PUBLISHING CO., INC.
645 NEW YORK AVENUE
HUNTINGTON, NEW YORK 11743

Copyright © 1977 by
ROBERT E. KRIEGER PUBLISHING COMPANY, INC.

Printed in the United States of America

**Library of Congress Cataloging in Publication Data**
Martin, James Kirby, 1943-
  American Revolution.

  Includes index.
  SUMMARY: Examines the degree to which everyday Americans representing specific social groups participated in and benefited from the American Revolution.

  1. United States—Politics and government—Revolution, 1775-1783. 2. United States—Social conditions—To 1865. [1. United States—Politics and government—Revolution, 1775-1783. 2. United States—Social conditions—To 1865] I. Stabaus, Karen R., joint author. II. Title.
E210.M35          973.3          76-18740
ISBN 0-88275-397-5

*For KENNETH L. CULVER*

*Historian,*

*Scholar,*

*Colleague,*

*and Friend*

James Kirby Martin and Karen R. Stubaus are members of the Department of History of Rutgers University. Previously Martin has written *Men in Rebellion: Higher Governmental Leaders and the Coming of the American Revolution* (1973), and he has edited *Interpreting Colonial America: Selected Readings* (1973), and *The Human Dimensions of Nation Making: Essays on Colonial and Revolutionary America* (1976). Stubaus is currently completing research for a study on crime, society, and culture in colonial Virginia.

# CONTENTS

# INTRODUCTION

Students and professional historians alike want to know much more than just what happened in history; they also want to know why it happened. The memorization of facts is useless unless those facts are somehow aligned, brought together, and interpreted in a meaningful fashion. In investigating particular historical epochs, then, we must search constantly for cause and effect relationships; we must consider how one series of events influences others; we must take short- and long-term factors into account; and we must decide whether individuals or impersonal forces lie at the heart of historical problems, as those problems constantly affect the unfolding drama of history and contemporary society.

For instance, the bare facts of the American Revolution are well known. Thirteen angry colonies rebelled against the mother country of Great Britain in 1776; representatives from each of the provinces signed the Declaration of Independence. Those representatives committed nearly three million Americans to the War for Independence. American leaders rejected Great Britain's constitutional monarchy, establishing in its stead a new system of government predicated upon popular sovereignty and republican principles. Eventually, delegates to the Constitutional Convention of 1787 gathered in Philadelphia from the several states and culminated Revolutionary activity by providing for a national government upon which to construct the future of the struggling United States among the nations of the world.

But beyond such skeletal statements lies the far more complex matter of interpretation. What actually "caused" the American Revolution? Did it result from essentially political, social, or economic forces? What was its ideological basis? What role did special interests play in the movement toward rebellion? Were individuals or events more important in bringing on and resolving the conflict?

At the center of the issue of causation are the three million people who resided in the thirteen British mainland colonies. John Adams, the Massachusetts radical whose career as a Revolutionary leader climaxed in

1

his election as the second president of the United States, understood the importance of the people in explaining causes and consequences. "The Revolution," wrote Adams in 1818, "was effected before the war commenced. The Revolution was in the minds and hearts of the people. . . . This radical change in the principles, opinions, sentiments, and affections of the people, was the real Revolution." To Adams, some profound alteration in the mentality of all Americans had occurred well before 1776. Historians know from looking at Adams's other writings that he was specifically referring to widespread colonial perceptions that ministers in England and their agents in America were threatening to destroy the liberties which the colonists should have been enjoying as Englishmen, such as the right to involvement in the decisions of government. Having enjoyed those liberties, the colonists were not about to give them up without a fight. Thus the minds and hearts of a united, freedom-loving people spurred everyone forward against the impending doom of imperial tyranny, or so claimed John Adams.

The Adams quotation is rich with information. Yet it is only one of many interpretive statements from participants in the Revolution. Less well-known but equally important, for instance, is the explanation of Dr. Benjamin Rush of Philadelphia, a man of the Enlightenment who believed that universal laws affecting human behavior could be uncovered through systematic study and scientific reasoning. Rush drew upon the principles of Enlightenment rationalism in observing during 1787 that "there is nothing more common, than to confound the terms of *American Revolution* with those of *the late American war*. The American war is over; but this is far from being the case with the American revolution. On the contrary," Rush observed, "nothing but the first act of the great drama is closed. It remains yet to establish and perfect our new forms of government; and to prepare the principles, morals, and manners of our citizens, for these forms of government, after they are established and brought to perfection." Obviously Rush did not see the people as leading the way in the creation of new governments; rather they would have to be educated over time to proper citizenship in the republic. For whatever reason, then, the people were simply not as central to Rush's interpretation as they were to Adams's.

The timing to Rush's assessment helps explain the difference. Rush was presenting his thoughts in the weeks before the assembling of the national Constitutional Convention in Philadelphia. He believed that the first central government of the new nation under the Articles of Confederation was too weak for the nation's good health. Rush was upset with the quarrelsome states, and he feared that internal instability, fomented by willful citizens who had gained too much power and authority in 1776, would undo the earlier successes of the experiment in republicanism. Thus he called for a stronger national government which, through its structural checks and balances, would stabilize internal political relations, hold down on popular excesses, and control the people until they had mastered the art of republican citizenship—defined as being willing to subordinate personal interests for the greater good of the state. For Rush the thrust toward popular sovereignty in revolution had gone too far; it had gotten out of hand in the drama's first act, and the only way to improve the remaining scenes was to control the people, a necessary part of the Revolutionary script.

Even though Adams and Rush were addressing different aspects of the Revolution, the one before and the other after 1776, they were not necessarily defining it differently. Both agreed that the Revolution was separate from the War for Independence. From Rush's other writings we know that he, like Adams, interpreted the coming Revolution as a struggle between liberty and tyranny. We also know that John Adams was not that different from Rush in thinking that the people had gotten out of hand and had gained too much decision-making power between 1775 and 1777 when so many new state constitutions provided for broader levels of popular participation in government. Both men thought that the people had been critical to the movement toward revolution, and both came to believe that the people would have to be put in a secondary position, under the guidance of "appropriate" leaders, until they proved themselves capable of virtuous, disinterested statesmanship, as befitted the citizens of any self-governing republic.

Indeed, a fundamental interpretive question about the American Revolution and its long-term impact on United States history arises in the context of the Adams-Rush observations. How central were the people themselves to the making and sustaining of the Revolution? Was the Revolution really of and for the people, or was it something less grandiose in reality? Who were the Revolutionaries and what were they after? In dedicating themselves to revolution, how sweeping were their accomplishments, and what have been the lasting effects of their achievements (or shortcomings)? In short, whose Revolution was it?

One form of widely-accepted interpretation holds that the people were at the core of the Revolution. Yet numerous modern historians, in studying the extensive letters, newspapers, pamphlets, and other materials surviving from the eighteenth century, have not been as sanguine in their conclusions. While noting that varieties of peoples and interests were involved in the making of Revolutionary events, they also point out that many others were not. The Revolution may have represented much more than a simple linear process of proclaiming and sustaining freedom for all throughout the land.

Professional historians, in fact, have rarely explained the Revolution in linear terms. Early in the twentieth century, for example, a number of scholars described it as a two-fold movement in its relation to the people. In the words of Carl Becker, two questions predominated: "The first was whether essential colonial rights should be maintained; the second was by whom and by what methods they should be maintained. The first was the question of home rule; the second was the question . . . of who should rule at home." Becker argued that the bulk of the common people had few basic political rights before the Revolution. Rather it was the aristocratic provincial upper class which controlled local authority and kept the lower orders in their place by denying them access to the channels of political power. But through the movement to defend liberty from even higher authority in Britain, the people began to throw off their shackles; they turned against their upper-class provincial leaders and began to seize political rights, in the process gaining the ability to rule at home. For Becker the beginnings of the Revolution kicked off the movement for broadly-based popular inclusion in the political system, a movement toward democracy which culminated in Andrew Jackson and his Democratic Party of the 1820s and 1830s.

At first merely peripheral, the people eventually became central to the Revolutionary experience, according to Becker and other historians of the early twentieth century, among them J. Franklin Jameson, whose study *The American Revolution Considered as a Social Movement* is the source of one of the introductory readings in this volume. Jameson investigated the status of several different groups in Revolutionary America and concluded that the Revolution ushered in a torrent of progress for the common people, even for the nearly half-million black slaves who fell completely outside the pale of political liberty. The rhetoric of republicanism, argued Jameson, stifled aristocratic and enhanced democratic tendencies in early America, pushing everything in the direction of greater equality.

Interpretations by professional historians, however, rarely emphasize the same themes for long. Historical understanding is incremental; one interpretation leads to another. New interpretations may arise from the discovery of new sources or from an enhanced appreciation of old ones, or from a certain "present-mindedness," an overwhelming concern with making the past relevant to immediate issues. The decade of the 1950s, for example, was a time when Americans grappled with what they believed to be an international Communist plot to subvert freedom. Those nervous Cold War years, years when it seemed as though we had to "close ranks" and play down our internal disagreements, helped spur a thorough-going reinvestigation of the American past. What emerged was an American history filled with continuity, consensus, and agreement. It was an American history that had no place for what Jameson and other conflict historians had described as our formative patterns of internal struggle. Scholars of the fifties claimed that the poor, the disaffected, and the politically deprived had not been as numerous or as important to an understanding of the Revolution as conflict historians had argued. In fact, as Robert E. Brown explained in 1955, it had been "a revolution to preserve a social order rather than to change it," a movement not to achieve "a democratic society but of keeping the democracy they had, a democracy threatened by British imperialism."

Provincial Americans had created something quite unique during the prerevolutionary years, according to historians of the consensus group. They had constructed a society far different from that of Europe, a society in which there was no oppressive class structure, seemingly only the bucolic and harmonious world of the freehold farmer and his devoted family. The bulk of adult white males not only had the franchise, but voted and participated in all forms of provincial political decision-making. It almost seemed as though Becker, Jameson, and their peers had misread the sources, for the consensus historians held that Americans had always been united in the struggle to defend freedom from the tyranny of imperialism, whether in its eighteenth- or its twentieth-century forms. The only struggle of importance during the 1760s and 1770s had been against Great Britain, an external struggle in which all Americans freely joined.

One outgrowth of this purging of the past was a careful reinvestigation by some scholars of the mentality of the Revolutionaries. In writing his *Ideological Origins of the American Revolution* in the 1960s, Bernard Bailyn broke with the interpretive extremes of the consensus school of the fifties but accepted their dictum that an essential type of prerevolutionary American had existed. It thus seemed possible that there could also have existed a commonly-held ideology of revolution. What Bailyn discovered was an apparently pervasive provincial worldview. In a selection from his work which follows he describes and analyzes that worldview, the colonists' perceptions of reality, and relates those perceptions to what he calls the radicalizing force of the Revolution, the creation of institutions that recognized and sustained the open, participatory pre-revolutionary American society. The Revolution was a movement which fulfilled the tendencies of an already-liberated society, concluded Bailyn, not one which began the creation of fundamental liberation for the American people, as Jameson had previously argued.

By extension, other scholars joining the ranks of established historians during the 1960s found neither the internal conflict nor the internal consensus models wholly acceptable. They began to investigate the sources

in new ways devoting attention to the "historically silent," the vast bulk
of any population who rarely leave behind written records of their thoughts,
ideals, aspirations, and frustrations. These historians found that there was
often a gap between the recorded observations of those who produced
the literary records, usually the educated elite, and the reality of daily
life for the bulk of the population. They discovered a provincial society
that was becoming more and more stratified economically and politically
on the eye of the Revolution, one in which personal wealth played a large
role in determining how much of a voice citizens had in local decision-
making, and one which was deferential in the sense that the "better sort"
fully expected to wield power while the "lesser sort" voluntarily deferred
to higher wisdom. For some of these historians, the evidence suggested
the possibility for popularly-based social change through the Revolution,
a conclusion similar to that of the earlier conflict historians. These scholars,
however, held that the promise of profound social change had not been
fully realized because of the continuing power of certain established
leadership elites into and well beyond the decision for independence.

No one interpretive mood became dominant among these scholars, but
all wanted to know more about the role of the people in the Revolution.
Selections from the work of James Kirby Martin and Linda Grant De Pauw
complete this volume's presentation of general interpretations. In *Men in
Rebellion,* Martin analyzed patterns of leadership turnover and change
during the years just before the Revolution, finding a pattern of political
immobility which effectively kept leaders of local American communities
from holding the highest offices in the colonial governments. The resulting
frustration helped intensify the confrontation that was coming and helped
lead these "lesser officials" to mobilize the colonial population for resistance and rebellion, all of which resulted in unintended opportunities for
new levels of popular involvement in politics and government after 1776.

While Martin concentrates on the struggle between lesser and higher
elite leaders, Linda Grant De Pauw, in her essay "Land of the Unfree,"
presents evidence demonstrating that only 15 percent of the population,
the free white adult males, were beneficiaries of the "new openness" of
Revolutionary American society. The other 85 percent, black slaves,
women, minors, and propertyless poor, enjoyed little if any advancement
of their political or legal rights through the Revolution. What is important,
according to De Pauw, is that the Revolution was born with an inherent
paradox, a paradox epitomized by the slaveholding Thomas Jefferson
penning a Declaration of Independence which castigated King George III
for denying liberty and human happiness through tyrannical actions.

In any general interpretive effort, we must be aware that words and
promises of historical participants often differ radically from deeds, that

broadly-defined goals for society often are at sharp variance with the reality of conditions. Based on the general comments by Jameson, Bailyn, Martin, and De Pauw, there are no easy answers in drawing out the role of the people in the Revolution, but we might keep in mind a well-known debate that occurred in an exchange of letters between John Adams and his brilliant wife Abigail in the spring of 1776. While away from home John kept Abigail well informed of his efforts for independence, yet Abigail sensed her husband's blindspots and admonished him pointedly:

> I desire you would remember the Ladies, and be more generous and favorable to them than your ancestors. Do not put such unlimited power into the hands of the Husbands. Remember all Men would be tyrants if they could. If particular care and attention is not paid to the Ladies we are determined to foment a Rebellion, and will not hold ourselves bound by any Laws in which we have no voice, or Representation.

Abigail was hoping that the defense of liberty would include the establishment of basic political rights for women, but that was beyond the imagination of her husband John. He responded to Abigail two weeks later with mock seriousness:

> Depend upon it, We know better than to repeal our Masculine systems. . . . We dare not exert our Power in its full Latitude. . . . We have only the Name of Masters, and . . . I begin to think the British Ministry as deep as they are wicked. After stirring up Tories, Landjobbers, Trimmers, Bigots, Canadians, Indians, Negroes, Hanoverians, Hessians, Russians, Irish Roman Catholics, Scotch Renegades, at last they have stimulated         to demand new Privileges and threaten to rebel.

For some reason John Adams did not write in the missing word and explicitly include women among those trying to destroy liberty. But he did facetiously imply that they were involved in what he and others believed to be a deep-seated plot, indeed a conspiracy of tyranny which had to be stopped. Uncovering and putting an end to that conspiracy was his primary goal, and nothing else seemed to matter to him, not even, ironically, the expansion of basic human rights.

What, then, were the goals of the Revolutionary leaders? How far were they willing to go in instituting fundamental change? What were the needs of the everyday citizens who lived through the Revolution but were more often followers than leaders? Were the goals of the leaders and the citizens essentially the same or fundamentally different? Comparing and contrasting the Revolutionary leaders with the people at large is one fruitful way to get the answers to these questions.

To facilitate the interpretive process, four separate but inter-related

topical sections are contained in this volume beyond the overview statements. The first, focusing on the people, Revolutionary crowds, and
violence as a form of popular participation in resistance to Great Britain,
juxtaposes essays by Gordon S. Wood and Jesse Lemisch. At one time,
scholars argued that mobs represented irrational collections of momentarily-
crazed individuals who mindlessly destroyed property and human lives
while under the influence of demagogic leaders. Modern analysts of crowd
behavior, among them Wood and Lemisch, have overturned that view,
finding that crowds were purposeful in intent, not particularly excessive
in their destruction of property, rarely interested in taking human lives,
and most often working to accomplish specific goals that would protect
group interests.

In fact, this latter point is essential in understanding the people and
the Revolution. Why did mob actions occur? What interests were the
crowds seeking to represent? Specific goals quite often depended upon the
types of individuals who participated in mob activities. For Wood, Revolutionary mobs tended to represent cross-sections of communities; crowd
violence was just one of many forms of confrontation in general resistance to British policy. As does Bailyn, Wood suggests that the fight to
preserve liberty against tyranny, rather than internal class conflict, best
explains Revolutionary mob violence.

While Wood indicates that crowds came together for action against
external (British) threats, Jesse Lemisch, in concentrating on the "Jack
Tars," the numerous merchant seamen in America's port towns, claims
that Revolutionary mobs were protesting economic deprivation and
political oppression. Writing within the so-called "New Left" school,
Lemisch documents the major part that seamen took in Revolutionary
incidents of violence, and he concludes that Jack Tar's behavior expressed
a sense of injustice and outrage against exploitive leaders everywhere, not
just in Britain. Since the individuals making up the mobs lacked political
rights of any kind, crowd action was their only effective alternate means of
demanding that the burdens of the poor and powerless be lifted. Merchant
seamen, then, worked as much to gain protection from the community
as they did to protect the community.

Given Wood's and Lemisch's explanations, what seems the most appropriate way to interpret crowd violence? Was it consensus or conflict
which brought the mobs out? Would crowd action have been necessary if
political rights had been more evenly distributed, or was the defense of
liberty the most important factor? What other explanations might there be
for the waves of crowd violence during the course of the Revolution? What
were the people trying to say about themselves, their society, and the
problems they faced? And finally, what impact did crowd violence have?

Did it help bring change for the people?

While crowds of free white citizens, no matter how personally deprived, voiced their grievances, black Americans in the Revolutionary years rarely had that opportunity. Afro-Americans were laboring under the yoke of chattel slavery, were being defined as property, at the very time that white Americans were shouting about Britain's campaign to foist political slavery on all colonists. Most historians agree that the Revolution's fixation on the defense of liberty had positive short- and long-term effects on the victims of the "peculiar institution," but the institution nonetheless remained intact. The Revolution, despite the Declaration of Independence and the doctrine that "all men are created equal," did not push very far toward eradicating human bondage from American soil. There was a gnawing gap between words and deeds.

At least 95 percent of all blacks, one-fifth of the American population, were slaves in late colonial America. All but 4 percent lived south of Pennsylvania and New Jersey, a region where the drive against human bondage showed no appreciable gains during the Revolution. How did the role of blacks and the problem of institutionalized slavery relate to the goals and ideals of the Revolution? How did slaves respond to Revolutionary conditions? Was the thinking of whites in regard to Afro-Americans modified at all in adjusting the ideology of liberty to the reality of the peculiar institution? The section on "Chattel Slavery for Blacks and the Revolution," which includes selections by Benjamin Quarles and Winthrop D. Jordan, can help answer these questions.

Most Americans know about Lincoln's Emancipation Proclamation, but few have heard of Lord Dunmore's 1775 Proclamation. Dunmore, the last royal governor of Virginia, encouraged slave resistance to rebellious colonial planters as a means of reestablishing imperial control in Virginia. Quarles looks at the crisis caused by Dunmore's Proclamation and the ways in which hundreds of blacks joined British forces in what might be described as "unpatriotic" behavior, given that black slaves who fought against Britain later on in the War for Independence quite often gained their freedom as a reward. But was it unpatriotic? How else could blacks have expressed their discontent with slavery? What does the fundamental blindness about slavery in the provinces tell us about the Revolutionary goals of those leading the movement against Britain?

While Quarles investigates an aspect of black resistance, Winthrop Jordan looks at white attitudes toward blacks in Revolutionary America. He explores the ways in which environmentalist-oriented Revolutionaries, such as Dr. Benjamin Rush, argued against what some eighteenth-century whites claimed was the inherent inferiority of blacks, claims used quite often by some individuals with vested interests to justify slavery for blacks while demanding liberty for whites. The environmentalists insisted that by changing the surroundings of an individual, it was demonstrable that presumed signs of innate inferiority were simply the products of prejudicial treatment and brutalizing plantation life. When slaves became free, the environmentalists maintained, they quickly showed their talents and abilities.

Thus the debate covered by Jordan held potential significance for the unfree black community in Revolutionary America. What does that debate reveal about the range of social commitments in the minds of free Revolutionaries? Did all of the talk mean anything in terms of improving the lot of chattel slaves living during an era of heightened concern about liberty?

The literature on slavery in America is enormous when compared with that on the changing status of women, the focus of the fourth section. Only in recent years have historians pushed beyond the so-called nineteenth-century "cult of domesticity" and begun to relate their findings to the women of the American Revolution. Mary Beth Norton and John Todd White have investigated two different groups of women in Revolutionary America; White has looked at the "camp followers" of the Continental Army, while Norton has written on loyalist women. Together their essays consider the possibilities for changing roles for women in late eighteenth-century America, keeping in mind, of course, the context of a male-oriented culture, about which Abigail Adams so vehemently complained.

The evidence on women "camp followers" of the Revolution indicates that they were, for the most part, from the economically-deprived classes. It was common military practice for women to travel with eighteenth-century armies in non-combatant status. Some women were not merely followers but were actually "on the ration," or paid to perform such chores as washing, sewing, cooking, burying the dead, nursing, and scavengering the enemy's dead after battle for needed clothing and supplies. Britain's army normally had a much higher proportion of women on the ration than did Washington's Continental forces, but the latter group is the focus of White's investigation. An impression of female hardiness, determined participation, and independence emerges from White's evidence. Did army life for the camp followers involve just another version of domestic duty, or did it mean a new measure of personal freedom, especially for those American women who crossed over traditional boundaries and entered the male-dominated world of field combat? Was this a possible beginning in the quest for full equality for women? Or were the results too limited to conclude that the general call to liberty meant anything for women's rights?

Mary Beth Norton, in her essay on loyalist women, is reluctant to conclude that the status of women improved during the age of the Revolution. In fact, her data suggest that women's roles in colonial America were more rigidly constrained than had previously been suspected, and that the Revolution and the ideology of republicanism may have worked to stifle nascent women's rights efforts by stressing "republican motherhood," defined as the obligation of patriotic women to raise dutiful sons willing to sacrifice personal needs and desires for the greater good of the republican community. At least loyalist women were spared that role, since it grew out of the provincial version of the ideology of liberty and republicanism.

Norton's work on loyalist women leads into the final topical area, that of "The Exclusion of the Loyalists." Loyalists comprised approximately one-third of the total population of the colonies on the eve of the Revolution. Either openly or covertly, they maintained their heretofore-accepted attachment to the Empire. Even before the War for Independence, rebellious Americans applied the stinging epithet "tory" to those not in agreement with them, comparing the loyalists to the politically-blind and unquestioningly-loyal followers of earlier English monarchs. Loyalists were mistreated, often humiliated in public, driven from their homes, and in some cases sentenced to death—and all in the name of liberty.

In selections from two studies of the loyalist phenomenon, William H. Nelson and Wallace Brown look at these individuals, their personal trials, and the reasons why they faced humiliating treatment as dissenters from the Revolution. Nelson finds that, as a group, they were more afraid of their neighbors in America than they were of British policies. What did they have to fear: An uncompromising Revolutionary leadership backed by the kinds of crowds Wood describes? The intolerance which the Revolutionary situation bred? Why were loyalists unable to organize themselves or halt the drift of events toward open rebellion when they were so numerous a part of the population?

For those loyalists whose allegiance became known to American rebels, Brown points out, liberty of person, conscience, and property ceased to have any meaning. "Patriotic" communities actively purged friends and neighbors who were loyalists as a pattern of brutal oppression swept through the Revolutionary countryside. But why this fierce need for communal consensus? What drove the people of the Revolution to extreme acts of persecution? Was liberty only meant to be for some of the people some of the time? Was the course of America's postrevolutionary history thus cast as a matter of securing liberty for more of the people more of the time?

Investigating these groups while keeping in mind the general interpretations contained in the first four selections should encourage students to evaluate the nature and significance of the American Revolution, not only as it occurred two centuries ago but as it has left its mark upon those centuries. In looking at the poor and disaffected, blacks in slavery, women, loyalists, and the leaders of the Revolution, we should gain a sense of that movement's inner dynamics, of its strengths and weaknesses, its achievements and blind spots, keeping in mind of course that the Revolution was as constrained by its times as we are by ours. It is unlikely that any interpretation will ever be considered final, but each person must seek to place the role of the people in perspective by asking, quite simply, "Whose Revolution?"

# The Historians' Overview

J. FRANKLIN JAMESON (1859–1937), a pioneer among modern professional historians, stressed economic factors as vital to an understanding of the American Revolution. To Jameson, the separation from Great Britain and the internal political upheaval had far-reaching social ramifications that led to significant alterations in many aspects of American life. Taken as a whole these changes comprised a true social revolution in late eighteenth-century America. Jameson summarized these views in a series of lectures given at Princeton University in 1926 marking the one-hundred and fiftieth anniversary of the Declaration of Independence. Later published under the title *The American Revolution Considered as a Social Movement,* the first lecture focused on the changing status of persons, central to any analysis of the people and the Revolution.

# The Revolution and the Status of Persons

Fifty years ago, and even a hundred years ago, there had become fixed in the public mind the notion that, because in the period of the Revolution there were many heroic characters and deeds, the whole American population of that time was heroic. It is pleasant to think well of a whole generation of those who have preceded us, and especially pleasant to glorify them if they were our ancestors. It may seem harmless, but when it is done in terms of comparison with later generations it is not altogether wholesome. It is not wholesome because it is not just. Nothing can be more certain than that, if we consider the whole nation and not merely the individual instances of heroic character and conduct, the patriotism of 1861, on both sides, was much more widely extended and more ardent than the much-lauded patriotism of 1776, and that of 1918 more pervasive, more enlightened, and more pure than either. How could we expect it to be otherwise, when we consider carefully the circumstances of the time? Let us distinguish between the heroes

From J. Franklin Jameson, The *American Revolution Considered as a Social Movement.* With a New Introduction by Frederick B. Tolles (Princeton Paperback, 1967), pp. 5–26. Reprinted by permission of Princeton University Press.

who fought and suffered and made every sacrifice to bring into existence a new nation, and the population at large, of whom so great a proportion were, as a matter of fact, however we may excuse them, provincial-minded, dubious in opinion, reluctant to make any sacrifices, half-hearted in the glorious cause. All honor to the heroes, and they were many.

We sit here in the Promised Land,
  That flows with Freedom's honey and milk;
But 'twas they won it, sword in hand,
  Making the nettle danger soft for us as silk.

But let us not forget that a large part of their heroism had to be expended in overcoming difficulties which need not have existed but for the slackness and indifference of their fellows. For instance, no episode of the history of the Revolution affords a finer example of patriotic sacrifice than the winter's encampment at Valley Forge; but why were the sufferings at Valley Forge encountered? Simply because the country at large, with whatever excuses, did not support the war, and the army which was waging it, with any approach to the ardor which was shown in 1861, on both sides, or in 1918. Clothes and shoes and blankets and tents were lacking. Who does not know what would happen if an American army of the present day were found to be destitute even of chocolate drops? It would not be three days before the metropolitan dailies would be voicing loudly a nation's wrath, and car-loads of chocolate drops would be rushed promptly to every camp. Let us be fair to the moderns, and not fabricate an imaginary golden age in the undeveloped America of 1776 . . . .

It is to be wished that in the coming commemorations and in our future thinking we may consider the American Revolution in broader aspects than simply the political and the military. Fifty years ago, it was these that engrossed attention, and indeed most that has been written since then about the Revolution has been narrowly confined to these two aspects, the political and the military, including of late the naval. Every move in the political struggle for independence from Great Britain, every action of the Continental Congress, has been described over and over again. Every battle and every skirmish in that long and dragging war has had its historian, or has been the theme of meticulous articles or controversial pamphlets. Meanwhile, even in this age when social history is so much in fashion all over the world, few writers have concerned themselves with the social aspects of our American revolutionary history.

How different is it with the Frenchmen's study of the great French Revolution! Forty or fifty years ago they were in much the same state as we: every move of the politicians, every picturesque happening in Paris, every march or engagement of the revolutionary armies, was eagerly chronicled by intelligent but more or less conventional historians; but in more recent years the horizon of the French historians of their revolution has broadened, and more attention has been given to the prodigious effects of the French Revolution upon the constitution of French society than to the political events, more to the march of the revolutionary battalions, and quite as much to the progress of the revolution in the provinces as to the dramatic events that marked its development in Paris. The result has been that the French Revolution is now seen in its true proportions and effects, not simply as the downfall of monarchy or the securing of equal political rights for all individuals, but chiefly as a social movement, French and European, of vast dimensions and of immense significance.

Perhaps some may be moved to say at once: But this is precisely to ignore the most salient contrast between the American Revolution and the French. The men of our Revolution, they will say, were neither levellers nor theorists. Their aims were distinctly political, not social. They fought for their own concrete rights as Englishmen, not for the abstract rights of man, nor for liberty, equality, and fraternity. The French rose in revolt against both a vicious political system and a vicious social system. With enthusiastic ardor they proceeded to sweep away abuses of all sorts, and to create, not simply a new government, but a new France and indeed, to their own imaginations, a new heaven and a new earth. That they cared more for the social than for the political results of the Revolution was evident when, after a few years, believing it impossible to retain both, they resigned political freedom and threw themselves into the arms of the young Corsican who gave promise of preserving for them their new social system. Not so, it will be said, the Anglo-Saxon. He had no wish to destroy or to recast his social system. He sought for political freedom, but he had no mind to allow revolution to extend itself beyond that limited sphere. As Burke said, he was "taught to look with horror on those children of their country who are prompted rashly to hack that aged parent to pieces and put him into the kettle of magicians, in hopes that by their poisonous weeds and wild incantations they may regenerate the paternal constitution."

It is indeed true that our Revolution was strikingly unlike that of France, and that most of those who originated it had no other than a political programme, and would have considered its work done when political independence of Great Britain had been secured. But who can say to the waves of revolution: Thus far shall we go and no farther? The various fibres of a nation's life are knit together in great complexity. It is impossible to sever some without also loosening others, and setting them free to combine anew in widely different forms. The Americans were much more conservative than the French. But their political and social systems, though both were, as the great orator said, still in the gristle and not yet hardened into the bone of manhood, were too intimately connected to permit that the one should remain unchanged while the other was radically altered. The stream of revolution, once started, could not be confined within narrow banks, but spread abroad upon the land. Many economic desires, many social aspirations were set free by the political struggle, many aspects of colonial society profoundly altered by the forces thus let loose. The relations of social classes to each other, the institution of slavery, the system of land-holding, the course of business, the forms and spirit of the intellectual and religious life, all felt the transforming hand of revolution, all emerged from under it in shapes advanced many degrees nearer to those we know. . . .

Meantime we might profitably consider for a moment whether it is intrinsically probable that our revolution was unlike other popular revolutions, in having no social results flowing from the political upheaval. Is there such a thing as a natural history of revolutions? Nation differs from nation, and age from age, but there are some uniformities in human nature, some natural sequences recurrently presenting themselves in human history. Not all political revolutions, it is true, have had important social consequences. One notable variety of revolution is that whereby one reigning individual or one small group of individuals holding supreme power is supplanted by another individual or small group, without any serious alteration of the system. Such are those "palace revolutions" whereby Jehu the son of Nimshi succeeds Jehoram the son of Ahab, or the tsar Alexander supplants the tsar Paul, without more disturbance of the social system than when "Amurath to Amurath succeeds" in a wholly peaceable manner. But it is the other variety, popular revolutions, which we have in mind. This is the variety which figures most largely in modern history. A popular revolution usually consists in the transfer of political power from the hands of a smaller into those of a larger mass of the citizens, or from one great section of the population to another. As the result of such a revolution, we expect to see the new group exercising its new-found power in accordance with its own interests or desires, until, with or without fixed intention of so doing, it alters the social system into something according better with its own ideals. . . .

If then it is rational to suppose that the American Revolution had some social consequences, what would they be likely to be? It would be natural to reply that it depends on the question, who caused the Revolution, and that therefore it becomes important to inquire what manner of men they were, and what they would be likely, consciously or unconsciously, to desire. In reality, the matter is not quite so simple as that. Allowance has to be made for one important fact in the natural history of revolutions, and that is, as they progress, they tend to fall into the hands of men holding more advanced or extreme views, less and less restrained by traditional attachment to the old order of things. Therefore the social consequences of a revolution are not necessarily shaped by the conscious or unconscious desires of those who started it, but more likely by the desires of those who came into control of it at later stages of its development. . . .

Or again, take the French Revolution. Everyone knows how its history is marked by distinct successive periods, in each of which the control is exercised by a group more radical and extreme than its predecessors; and the same has been true of the great Russian revolution. Now, widely as our American Revolution differed from these, do not let us suppose that it escaped every trait of conformity to the natural history of such movements. Certain it is that, in some of our states at least, it fell ultimately into quite other hands than those that set it in motion.

Well, then, we may ask, who were in favor of the Revolution, and who were against it? The answer of course varies with the different stages of its development. In 1774 the partisans of American independence were very few, though there had long been those who thought, in an academic way, that it would soon take place. In most years after 1776 the partisans of American independence were the great majority. But what sort of man became a Tory as it gradually became necessary to take sides? What sort of man became a Whig? As a matter of course, almost all persons who enjoyed office under the Crown became Tories, and these were a large number. In an age when the king's turnspit was a member of Parliament, and under a king whose chief means of political action was the distribution of offices, office-holders were certain to be numerous, and their pay was, in proportion to the wealth of the country and the work they had to do, much greater than it is now. If the natural desire of all mankind to hold on to a lucrative office (a desire which is said sometimes to influence political action even in this age) did not make an office-holder a Tory, there was another motive arising from the fact that he had been appointed and had sworn to execute the laws, and might therefore feel in duty bound to obey the instructions, of the ministers in England. As for the merchants, many, who had extensive interests that were imperilled by rebellion, adhered to the royal cause. But on the whole the great body of the merchants of the thirteen colonies were Whigs, for of the deep underlying causes, which for a generation had been moving the American mind in the direction of independence, none was so potent, according to all the best testimony, as the parliamentary restrictions on the trade of the colonies. Among farmers many of the richest took the royalist side. Probably most Episcopalians did so, except in the South. Everywhere the debtor class was, as was natural, and as had been true the whole world over, mainly on the side of revolution.

If we speak of professions, we should note that probably most of the clergy were Whigs, with the exception of nearly all the clergymen of the Church of England in the northern colonies. Most lawyers were Whigs, but most of the most eminent and of those enjoying the largest practice were Tories. John Adams says that, of the eight lawyers who had an important practice before the Superior Court of Massachusetts at the time of the Stamp Act, only Otis and he were Whigs ten years later. One of the others had died, and the remaining five were Tories. Among physicians the proportion of Tories was quite as large as among lawyers.

A word as to race and nationality. Colonists who had very recently arrived from England were likely to take the Tory side. Immigrants from Scotland, also, were usually Tories. A hundred and fifty years ago the Scots at home were among the warmest of Tories; Hume's *History of England* is typical of their feelings. Perhaps, too, their well-known clannishness gave them, in America, the position of aliens who held together, and would not assimilate with the rest of the population. Of the Irish, on the other hand, and those of the Scotch-Irish stock, Protestants from the north of Ireland, it is customary to hold that they were warmly and by vast majority on the side of revolution. It is not so certain. Industrious efforts have been made to show that they formed the backbone of the Revolutionary army—efforts partly based on a misinterpretation of a single passage in Joseph Galloway's testimony before a committee of the House of Commons. On the other hand, I have observed that, in the two large lists of Loyalist claimants that give the country of birth, 146 out of 1358 claimants, or eleven percent, say that they were born in Ireland—a larger number than were born in England. Yet in Pennsylvania, where the proportion of Irish or Scotch-Irish population was greatest, it was unquestionably their influence that carried the state for independence, at the same time breaking the power in state affairs of the Philadelphia conservatives, and bestowing upon the state a radically democratic constitution. In all the colonies the Germans generally adhered to the party of independence, but not with great ardency.

As is usually the case, the revolutionary side was more frequently espoused by young men, the conservative cause by their elders. There were not a few conspicuous cases, such as that of Sir John Randolph, the king's attorney-general in Virginia, and his son Edmund Randolph, in which the son adopted the former, the father the latter cause, and other cases, like that of Samuel and Josiah Quincy, in which an elder and a younger brother were thus divided. Among all the leaders of the Revolution, very few were forty-five years old in 1775; most were under forty. But think for a moment of the leaders of the French Revolution —Robespierre thirty-one years old when the Revolution began, Danton thirty, Camille Desmoulins, twenty-seven, Collot-d'Herbois thirty-nine, Couthon thirty-three, Lebas twenty-four, Saint-Just twenty-one—and we shall see cause

to be glad that our Revolution was carried through by men who, though still young, had at any rate reached their full maturity of thought and of character.

If we should investigate the Tory party in the several colonies in detail, we should be forced to the conviction that, in New England, it comprised in 1775 a very great share, probably more than half, of the most educated, wealthy, and hitherto respected classes. In March 1776, when Howe evacuated Boston, eleven hundred refugees sailed away with him. These eleven hundred, and the thousand or more who subsequently followed them, bore away perhaps a majority of the old aristocracy of Massachusetts. The act of banishment which the state legislature passed in 1778, to punish the Tories, includes among its three hundred-odd names some representatives of most of the families which had been distinguished in the earlier days of the colony. The loss of this important element, cultivated, experienced, and public-spirited, was a very serious one. It is true that many Tories returned after the war, but their fortunes were usually much broken, and they could never regain their influence. In New England, in short, it appears that the Revolution brought new strata everywhere to the surface.

In New York it seems probable that, in the height of the war at least, the bulk of the property-owners belonged to the Tory party, and it was strong also among the middle classes of the towns and among the country population. On the large manorial estates the tenant farmers sided with their landlords if they took sides at all. The city of New York and the county of

Westchester were strongly Tory during at least the period of the British occupation, and Westchester very likely before. So were Staten Island and the three counties of Long Island.

In Pennsylvania it is probable that during the critical years of the war, at least, the majority of the population was on the side of the Crown, and that majority seems to have included many persons of eminence, and many Quakers. On the other hand, as is well known, the Virginian aristocracy in general, living somewhat remote from the influence of the royal officials, upon their secluded estates, were full of the spirit of local independence. Quite unlike their New England compeers, they took the Whig side, and that almost unanimously. It was the Virginian planters who formed the local committees, seized from the outset the control of the movement, and made it impossible for loyalty to show itself in concerted or effective action. And it is well known how numerous and active were the Tories in the Carolinas. But, says Dr. Ramsay, speaking of South Carolina, "Beside their superiority in numbers, there was an ardour and enthusiasm in the friends of Congress which was generally wanting in the advocates for royal government." Is not this a most significant touch? After all the evidence as to classes and numbers—for perhaps there were a hundred thousand Loyalist exiles, to say nothing of the many more who did not emigrate—the ultimate success of the American cause might well seem to us a miracle. But the fact remains that the Revolutionary party knew what they wanted. They had a definite programme, they had boldness and resolution, while those averse to

independence were divided in their counsels, and paralyzed by the timidity which naturally cleaves to conservative minds. The first scientific observer of political revolutions, Thucydides, pointed out, and every subsequent revolution has accentuated his words, that in such times boldness and evergy are more important requisites to success than intelligence or all other qualities put together. This is the secret of the whole matter. "There was an ardour and enthusiasm in the friends of Congress which was generally wanting in the advocates for royal government."

All things considered, it seems clear that in most states the strength of the revolutionary party lay most largely in the plain people, as distinguished from the aristocracy. It lay not in the mob or rabble, for American society was overwhelmingly rural and not urban, and had no sufficient amount of mob or rabble to control the movement, but in the peasantry, substantial and energetic though poor, in the small farmers and frontiersmen. And so, although there were men of great possessions like George Washington and Charles Carroll of Carrollton who contributed a conservative element, in the main we must expect to see our social changes tending in the direction of levelling democracy.

It would be aside from the declared purpose of these lectures to dwell upon the political effects which resulted from the victory of a party constituted in the manner that has been described. There are, however, some political changes that almost inevitably bring social changes in their wake. Take, for instance, the expansion of the suffrage. The status in which the electoral franchise was left at the end of the Revolutionary period fell far short of complete democracy. Yet during the years we are considering the right of suffrage was much extended. The freeholder, or owner of real estate, was given special privileges in four of the new state constitutions, two others widened the suffrage to include all owners of either land or personal property to a certain limit, and two others conferred it upon all tax-payers. Now if in this lecture we are considering especially the status of persons, we must take account of the fact that the elevation of whole classes of people to the status of voters elevates them also in their social status. American society in the colonial period had a more definite and stable organization than it ever has had since the Revolution. . . .

Rip Van Winkle, whose sleep bridged just these years, found the atmosphere of his village radically altered. Jeremy Belknap of New Hampshire, writing in 1792, after remarking on the effect of the Revolution in calling the democratic power into action and repressing the aristocratic spirit, confesses that in the new state "the deficiency of persons qualified for the various departments in the Government has been much regretted, and by none more than by those few who know how public business ought to be conducted." In that entertaining Virginian autobiography, the *Life* of the Reverend Devereux Jarratt, after speaking of the habit in that writer's youth, among the plain people with whom he grew up, of regarding gentle-folk as beings of a superior order, he says in 1794:

But I have lived to see a vast alteration in this respect and the contrary extreme prevail. In our high republican times there is more levelling than ought to be, consistent with good government. I have as little notion of oppression and tyranny as any man, but a due subordination is essentially requisite in every government. At present there is too little regard and reverence paid to magistrates and persons in public office; and whence do this regard and irreverence originate but from the notion and practice of levelling? An idea is held out to use that our present government and state are far superior to the former, when we were under the royal administration; but my age enables me to know that the people are not now by half so peacefully and quietly governed as formerly; nor are the laws, perhaps by the tenth part, so well executed. And yet I know the superiority of the present government. In theory it is certainly superior; but in practice it is not so. This can arise from nothing so much as from want of a proper distinction between the various orders of the people.

Similar voices come from North Carolina, where one stout conservative laments the "extension of that most delicate and important right [of suffrage] to every biped of the forest," and another declares that: "Anyone who has the least pretence to be a gentleman is suspected and borne down *per ignobile vulgus*—a set of men without reading, experience, or principle to govern them." In fact, the sense of social change pervaded the country. A writer in South Carolina says, quite in the spirit of these lectures, "There is nothing more common than to confound the terms of the American Revolution with those of the late American war. The American war is over, but this is far from being the case with the American revolution. On the contrary, nothing but the first act of the great drama is closed." . . .

We might also expect the equilitarian or humane spirit to show itself in alterations of the laws respecting redemptioners or indented servants. Those laws, however, seem not to have been changed in the Revolutionary period. We may infer that the laws protecting the interests of such persons, a very numerous class in the years just preceding the Revolution, either were, or were deemed to be, adequate already for their humane purpose, and that the status of the indented, who after all had but a few years to serve and then would have all the rights of poor people, was not regarded as seriously unsatisfactory.

A far more serious question, in any consideration of the effect of the American Revolution on the status of persons, is that of its influence on the institution of slavery, for at this time the contrast between American freedom and American slavery comes out, for the first time, with startling distinctness. It has often been asked: How could men who were engaged in a great and inspiring struggle for liberty fail to perceive the inconsistency between their professions and endeavors in that contest and their actions with respect to their bondmen? How could they fail to see the application of their doctrines respecting the rights of man to the black men who were held among them in bondage far more reprehensible than that to which they indignantly proclaimed themselves to have been subjected by the King of Great Britain?

At the time when the Revolution broke out there were about a half-million of slaves in the Thirteen Colonies, the figures probably running about as follows: 200,000 in Virginia, 100,000 in South Carolina, 70,000 or 80,000 each in Maryland and in North Carolina, 25,000 perhaps in New York, 10,000 in New Jersey, 6,000 in Pennsylvania, 6,000 in Connecticut, 5,000 in Massachusetts, 4,000 in Rhode Island. Slavery in the continental colonies at that time was no doubt less harsh than in the West Indies, and milder than it has been in many other countries and times. An English parson, preaching to a Virginian congregation in 1763, says: "I do you no more than justice in bearing witness, that in no part of the world were slaves ever better treated than, in general, they are in the colonies." But slavery is slavery, and already before the Revolution many hearts had been stirred against it. It is of course true that other influences than those of the American Revolution were abroad in the world at the same time which would surely work in some degree against the institution of human slavery. On the one hand Voltaire had raised a powerful, if at times a grating, voice in favor of a rational humanitarianism, and Rousseau had poured upon time-worn institutions the active solvent of abounding sentimentality. Quite at another extreme of human thought from them, Wesley and Whitefield had stirred the English nation into a warmth of religious feeling of which Methodism was only one result, and with it came a revived interest in all varieties of philanthropic endeavor.

There is no lack of evidence that, in the American world of that time, the analogy between freedom for whites and freedom for blacks was seen. If we are to select but one example of such evidence, the foremost place must surely be given to the striking language of Patrick Henry, used in 1773, when he was immersed in the struggle against

Great Britain. It is found in a letter which he wrote to one who had sent him a copy of Anthony Benezet's book on slavery.

It is not amazing [he says] that at a time, when the rights of humanity are defined and understood with precision, in a country above all others fond of liberty, that in such an age and in such a country we find men professing a religion the most humane, mild, gentle and generous, adopting a principle as repugnant to humanity as it is inconsistent with the Bible and destructive to liberty? . . . Would anyone believe I am the master of slaves of my own purchase! I am drawn along by the general inconvenience of living here without them. I will not, I can not justify it. However, culpable my conduct, I will so far pay my devoir to virtue, as to own the excellence and rectitude of her precepts, and lament my want of conformity to them. I believe a time will come when an opportunity will be offered to abolish this lamentable evil. Everything we can do is to improve it, if it happens in our day, if not, let us transmit to our descendants, together with our slaves, a pity for their unhappy lot, and an abhorrence of slavery. . . . It is a debt we owe to the purity of our religion, to show that it is at variance with that law which warrants slavery.

Along with many examples and expressions of individual opinion, we may note that organized efforts toward the removal or alleviation of slavery manifested in the creation of a whole group of societies for these purposes. The first anti-slavery society in this or any other country was formed on April 14, 1775, five days before the battle of Lexington, by a meeting at the Sun Tavern, on Second Street in Philadelphia. The members were mostly of the Society of Friends. The organization took the name of "The Society for the Relief of Free Negroes unlawfully held

in Bondage." In the preamble of their constitution they point out that "loosing the bonds of wickedness and setting the oppressed free, is evidently a duty incumbent on all professors of Christianity, but more especially at a time when justice, liberty, and the laws of the land are the general topics among most ranks and stations of men." The New York "Society for Promoting the Manumission of Slaves" was organized in 1785, with John Jay for its first president. In 1788 a society similar to these two was founded in Delaware, and within four years there were other such in Rhode Island, Connecticut, New Jersey, Maryland, and Virginia, and local societies enough to make at least thirteen, mostly in the slave-holding states.

In actual results of the growing sentiment, we may note, first of all, the checking of the importation of slaves, and thus of the horrors of the trans-Atlantic slave trade. The Continental Congress of 1774 had been in session but a few days when they decreed an "American Association," or non-importation agreement, in which one section read: "That we will neither import nor purchase any slave imported after the first day of December next, after which we will wholly discontinue the slave trade, and will neither be concerned in it ourselves, nor will we hire our vessels nor sell our commodities or manufactures to those who are concerned in it"; and the evidence seems to be that the terms of this agreement were enforced throughout the war with little evasion.

States also acted. Four months before this, in July 1774, Rhode Island had passed a law to the effect that all slaves thereafter brought into the colony should be free. The influence under which it was passed may be seen from the preamble. "Whereas," it begins, "the inhabitants of America are generally engaged in the preservation of their own rights and liberties, among which that of personal freedom must be considered as the greatest, and as those who are desirous of enjoying all the advantages of liberty themselves should be willing to extend personal liberty to others," etc. A similar law was passed that same year in Connecticut. Delaware prohibited importation in 1776, Virginia in 1778, Maryland in 1783, South Carolina in 1787, for a term of years, and North Carolina, in 1786, imposed a larger duty on each negro imported.

Still further, the states in which slaves were few proceeded, directly as a consequence of the Revolutionary movement, to effect the immediate or gradual abolition of slavery itself. Vermont had never recognized its existence, but Vermont was not recognized as a state. Pennsylvania in 1780 provided for gradual abolition, by an act which declared that no negro born after that date should be held in any sort of bondage after he became twenty-eight years old, and that up to that time his service should be simply like that of an indented servant or apprentice. Now what says the preamble of this act? That when we consider our deliverance from the abhorrent condition to which Great Britain has tried to reduce us, we are called on to manifest the sincerity of our professions of freedom, and to give substantial proof of gratitude, by extending a portion of our freedom to others, who, though of a different color, are the work of the same Al-

mighty hand. Evidently here also the leaven of the Revolution was working as a prime cause in this philanthropic endeavor.

The Superior Court of Massachusetts declared that slavery had been abolished in that state by the mere declaration of its constitution that "all men are born free and equal." In 1784 Connecticut and Rhode Island passed acts which gradually extinguished slavery. In other states, ameliorations of the law respecting slaves were effected even though the abolition of slavery could not be brought about. Thus in 1782 Virginia passed an act which provided that any owner might, by an instrument properly attested, freely manumit all his slaves, if he gave security that their maintenance should not become a public charge. It may seem but a slight thing, this law making private manumission easy where before it had been difficult. But it appears to have led in eight years to the freeing of more than ten thousand slaves, twice as great a number as were freed by reason of the Massachusetts constitution, and as many as there were in Rhode Island and Connecticut together when the war broke out.

That all was not done that might have been done for the removal or amelioration of slavery we cannot deny, nor that there was in many places a glaring contrast between the principles avowed by the men of the Revolution and their acts respecting slavery; yet very substantial progress was made, and that more was made in this period than in any other until a much later time may be taken as clear evidence of a pronounced influence of the Revolution upon the status of persons in the realm where that status stood most in need of amelioration.

Thus in many ways the successful struggle for the independence of the United States affected the character of American society by altering the status of persons. The freeing of the community led not unnaturally to the freeing of the individual; the raising of colonies to the position of independent states brought with it the promotion of many a man to a higher order in the scale of privilege or consequence. So far at any rate as this aspect of life in America is concerned, it is vain to think of the Revolution as solely a series of political or military events.

BERNARD BAILYN (b. 1922) has placed particular emphasis upon the Revolution as an intellectual movement, but not in the traditional manner of studying the history of ideas. Rather, in *Ideological Origins of the American Revolution* Bailyn stresses the importance of an emerging provincial worldview of a British ministerial conspiracy to destroy English liberties in America. This mindset became a radicalizing force by propelling Americans forward toward the creation and institutionalization of republican forms of government by means of the Revolution. While Jameson stressed the influence of the unenfranchised and underprivileged, Bailyn credits the ideology of liberty with transforming power. But has he pushed too far into the background possible energizing differences among the people (rich and poor, black and white, male and female, rebel and loyalist) for merely interpretive purposes?

# The Ideology of Liberty

What was essentially involved in the American Revolution was not the disruption of society, with all the fear, despair, and hatred that that entails, but the realization, the comprehension and fulfillment, of the inheritance of liberty and of what was taken to be America's destiny in the context of world history. The great social shocks that in the French and Russian Revolutions sent the foundations of thousands of individual lives crashing into ruins had taken place in America in the course of the previous century, slowly, silently, almost imperceptibly, not as a sudden avalanche but as myriads of individual changes and adjustments which had gradually transformed the order of society. By 1763 the great landmarks of European life—the church and the idea of orthodoxy, the state and the idea of authority: much of the array of institutions and ideas that buttressed the society of the *ancien régime*—had faded in their exposure to the open, wilderness environment of America. But until the disturbances of the 1760's these changes had not

Excerpted by permission of the author and publishers from *The Ideological Origins of the American Revolution* by Bernard Bailyn, Cambridge, Massachusetts: The Belknap Press of Harvard University Press, Copyright © 1967 by the President and Fellows of Harvard College. Footnotes omitted.

been seized upon as grounds for a reconsideration of society and politics. Often they had been condemned as deviations, as retrogressions back toward a more primitive condition of life. Then, after 1760—and especially in the decade after 1765—they were brought into open discussion as the colonists sought to apply advanced principles of society and politics to their own immediate problems.

The original issue of the Anglo-American conflict was, of course, the question of the extent of Parliament's jurisdiction in the colonies. But that could not be discussed in isolation. The debate involved eventually a wide range of social and political problems, and it ended by 1776 in what may be called the conceptualization of American life. By then Americans had come to think of themselves as in a special category, uniquely placed by history to capitalize on, to complete and fulfill, the promise of man's existence. The changes that had overtaken their provincial societies, they saw, had been good: elements not of deviance and retrogression but of betterment and progress; not a lapse into primitivism, but an elevation to a higher plane of political and social life than had ever been reached before. Their rustic blemishes had become the marks of a chosen people. "The liberties of mankind and the glory of human nature is in their keeping," John Adams wrote in the year of the Stamp Act. "America was designed by Providence for the theatre on which man was to make his true figure, on which science, virtue, liberty, happiness, and glory were to exist in peace."

The effort to comprehend, to communicate, and to fulfill this destiny was continuous through the entire Revolutionary generation—it did not cease, in fact, until in the nineteenth century its creative achievements became dogma. But there were three phases of particular concentration: the period up to and including 1776, centering on the discussion of Anglo-American differences; the devising of the first state governments, mainly in the years from 1776 to 1780; and the reconsideration of the state constitutions and the reconstruction of the national government in the last half of the eighties and in the early nineties. In each of these phases important contributions were made not only to the skeletal structure of constitutional theory but to the surrounding areas of social thought as well. But in none was the creativity as great, the results as radical and as fundamental, as in the period before Independence. It was then that the premises were defined and the assumptions set. It was then that explorations were made in new territories of thought, the first comprehensive maps sketched, and routes marked out. Thereafter the psycological as well as intellectural barriers were down. It was the most creative period in the history of American political thought. Everything that followed assumed and built upon its results. . . .

The colonists' attitude to the whole world of politics and government was fundamentally shaped by the root assumption that they, as Britishers, shared in a unique inheritance of liberty. The English people, they believed, though often threatened by despots who had risen in their midst, had managed to maintain, to a greater degree and for a longer period of time than any other people, a tradition of the successful control of power and of those evil tendencies of human nature that would prevent its proper uses.

In view of the natural obstacles that stood in the way of such a success and in view of the dismal history of other nations, this, as the colonists saw it, had been an extraordinary achievement. But it was not a miraculous one. It could be explained historically. The ordinary people of England, they believed, were descended from simple, sturdy Saxons who had known liberty in the very childhood of the race and who, through the centuries, had retained the desire to preserve it. But it had taken more than desire. Reinforcing, structuring, expressing the liberty-loving temper of the people, there was England's peculiar "constitution," described by John Adams, in words almost every American agreed with before 1763, as "the most perfect combination of human powers in society which finite wisdom has yet contrived and reduced to practice for the preservation of liberty and the production of happiness." . . .

By 1763, before any of the major problems of Anglo-American relations had appeared, the belief was widespread in America that while liberty had been better preserved in England than elsewhere in the Old World, the immediate circumstances in the home country were far from conducive to the continued maintenance of liberty— that it was not unreasonable to believe, in fact, that a new crisis of liberty might be approaching. Writings popular in the colonies insisted that the environment of eighteenth-century England was, to a dangerous degree, hostile to liberty: that Jacobite remnants flourished, that effeminizing lux-

ury and slothful negligence continued to soften the moral fiber of the nation, and that politics festered in corruption. Specifically, the colonists were told again and again that the prime requisite of constitutional liberty, an independent Parliament free from the influence of the crown's prerogative, was being undermined by the successful efforts of the administration to manipulate Parliamentary elections to its advantage and to impose its will on members in Parliament.

How widespread the fear was in America that corruption was ripening in the home country, sapping the foundations of that most famous citadel of liberty, may be seen not only in the general popularity of periodicals like *The Craftsman* and *Cato's Letters,* which repeatedly excoriated the degeneracy of the age and the viciousness of ministerial corruption, but in the deliberateness with which some of the most vituperative of the English jeremiads were selected for republication in the colonies. There is no more sustained and intense attack on the corruption of Augustan England than James Burgh's *Britain's Remembrancer: or, The Danger Not Over* . . . (London, 1746), which had been touched off by the shock of the 'Forty-five. Its perfervid denunciation of "our degenerate times and corrupt nation"—a people wallowing in "luxury and irreligion . . . venality, perjury, faction, opposition to legal authority, idleness, gluttony, drunkenness, lewdness, excessive gaming, robberies, clandestine marriages, breach of matrimonial vows, self-murders . . . a legion of furies sufficient to rend any state or empire that ever was in the world to pieces"— this blasting denunciation could scarcely have been improved upon by the most sulphurous of Puritan patriarchs. The pamphlet was reprinted by Franklin the year after its initial appearance; reprinted again the following year by another printer in Philadelphia; and reprinted still again in Boston in 1759. So too the lengthy lament, *An Estimate of the Manners and Principles of the Times,* written by the fashionable belletrist and Church of England preacher, Dr. John Brown, despairing of the prospects of liberty in England ("We are rolling to the brink of a precipice that must destroy us"), decrying the *"vain, luxurious,* and *selfish* EFFEMINACY" of the British people, and attributing the "weaken[ing of] the *foundations* of our *constitution"* to the deliberate corruption of the Commons by Robert Walpole, was reprinted in Boston in 1758, a year after its first publication.

Such charges were not allowed to dissipate. They were repeatedly reinforced by the testimony of direct experience. Letters from England expressed in personal terms what print impersonally conveyed—letters not only from such doctrinaire libertarians as Thomas Hollis but also from such undogmatic conservatives as the printer William Strahan, who wondered, he wrote David Hall in Philadelphia in 1763, whether England had "virtue enough to be saved from that deluge of corruption with which we have been so long overwhelmed." The same question had long since occurred to Americans visiting England for business, pleasure, or education. Lewis Morris, in London in 1735–36 to recover the political losses he had sustained in New York at the hands of Governor Cosby, returned home with so intense a disgust at the scenes he had beheld

that he took to poetry to relieve his feelings. His 700-line poem, "The Dream and Riddle" echoed the many despairing pamphlets, poems, and squibs published in London in the 1720's and early 1730's in ridiculing the justice of the English government ("Complaints if just are very shocking things; /And not encouraged in the courts of Kings"); the venality of the court (". . . our noble Prince's ear/Is open to complaints, and he will hear;/The difficulty's how to get them there"); the mores of shopkeepers ("The gaudy shops of this tumultuous hive/By several arts of cheating only thrive"); and the corruption of Parliament ("Both senates and their chosers vote for pay/ And both alike their liberty betray"). He ended with what would become a characteristic American response: "If bound unto that land of liberty/ I just described, then know it is not nigh [i.e., in England],/But lies far distant from this place somewhere/ Not in this, but some other hemisphere." . . .

It is the meaning imparted to the events after 1763 by this integrated group of attitudes and ideas that lies behind the colonists' rebellion. In the context of these ideas, the controversial issues centering on the question of Parliament's jurisdiction in America acquired as a group new and overwhelming significance. The colonists believed they saw emerging from the welter of events during the decade after the Stamp Act a pattern whose meaning was unmistakable. They saw in the measures taken by the British government and in the actions of officials in the colonies something for which their peculiar inheritance of thought had prepared them only too

well, something they had long conceived to be a possibility in view of
the known tendencies of history and
of the present state of affairs in England. They saw about them, with increasing clarity, not merely mistaken,
or even evil, policies violating the
principles upon which freedom rested,
but what appeared to be evidence of
nothing less than a deliberate assault
launched surreptitiously by plotters
against liberty both in England and in
America. The danger to America, it
was believed, was in fact only the
small, immediately visible part of the
greater whole whose ultimate mani-
festation would be the destruction of
the English constitution, with all the
rights and privileges embedded in it.

This belief transformed the meaning
of the colonists' struggle, and it added
an inner accelerator to the movement
of opposition. For, once assumed, it
could not be easily dispelled: denial
only confirmed it, since what conspirators profess is not what they believe; the ostensible is not the real; and
the real is deliberately malign.

It was this—the overwhelming evidence, as they saw it, that they were
faced with conspirators against liberty
determined at all costs to gain ends
which their words dissembled—that was
signaled to the colonists after 1763,
and it was this above all else that in the
end propelled them into Revolution....

In the light of such a conception
everything about the colonies and their
controversy with the mother country
took on a new appearance. Provincial-
ism was gone: Americans stood side by
side with the heroes of historic battles
for freedom and with the few remaining champions of liberty in the present.
What were once felt to be defects—

isolation, institutional simplicity, prim-
itiveness of manners, multiplicity of
religions, weakness in the authority of
the state—could now be seen as virtues,
not only by Americans themselves but
by enlightened spokesmen of reform,
renewal, and hope wherever they might
be—in London coffeehouses, in Parisian
*salons,* in the courts of German princes.
The mere existence of the colonists
suddenly became philosophy teaching
by example. Their manners, their morals, their way of life, their physical,
social, and political condition were
seen to vindicate eternal truths and to
demonstrate, as ideas and words never
could, the virtues of the heavenly city
of the eighteenth-century philosophers.

But the colonists' ideas and words
counted too, and not merely because
they repeated as ideology the familiar
utopian phrases of the Enlightenment
and of English libertarianism. What
they were saying by 1776 was familiar
in a general way to reformers and
illuminati everywhere in the Western
world; yet is was different. Words and
concepts had been reshaped in the
colonists' minds in the course of a
decade of pounding controversy—
strangely reshaped, turned in unfamil-
iar directions, toward conclusions they
could not themselves clearly perceive.
They found a new world of political
thought as they struggled to work out
the implications of their beliefs in the
years before Independence. It was a
world not easily possessed; often they
withdrew in some confusion to more
familiar ground. But they touched its
boundaries, and, at certain points,
probed its interior. Others, later—
writing and revising the first state constitutions, drafting and ratifying the
federal constitution, and debating in

detail, exhaustively, the merits of these efforts—would resume the search for resolutions of the problems the colonists had broached before 1776.

This critical probing of traditional concepts—part of the colonists' efforts to express reality as they knew it and to shape it to ideal ends—became the basis for all further discussions of enlightened reform, in Europe as well as in America. The radicalism the Americans conveyed to the world in 1776 was a transformed as well as a transforming force. . . .

In no obvious sense was the American Revolution undertaken as a social revolution. No one, that is, deliberately worked for the destruction or even the substantial alteration of the order of society as it had been known. Yet it was transformed as a result of the Revolution, and not merely because Loyalist property was confiscated and redistributed, or because the resulting war destroyed the economic bases of some people's lives and created opportunities for others that would not otherwise have existed. Seizure of Loyalist property and displacements in the economy did in fact take place, and the latter if not the former does account for a spurt in social mobility that led earlier arrivés to remark, "When the pot boils, the scum will rise." Yet these were superficial changes; they affected a small part of the population only, and they did not alter the organization of society.

What did now affect the essentials of organization—what in time would help permanently to transform them— were changes in the realm of belief and attitude. The views men held toward the relationships that bound them to each other—the discipline and

pattern of society—moved in a new direction in the decade before Independence.

Americans of 1760 continued to assume, as had their predecessors for generations before, that a healthy society was a hierarchical society, in which it was natural for some to be rich and some poor, some honored and some obscure, some powerful and some weak. And it was believed that superiority was unitary, and that the attributes of the favored—wealth, wisdom, power—had a natural affinity to each other, and hence that political leadership would naturally rest in the hands of the social leaders. Movement, of course, there would be: some would fall and some would rise; but manifest, external differences among men, reflecting the principle of hierarchical order, were necessary and proper, and would remain; they were intrinsic to the nature of things.

Circumstances had pressed harshly against such assumptions. The wilderness environment from the beginning had threatened the maintenance of elaborate social distinctions; many of them in the passage of time had in fact been worn away. Puritanism, in addition, and the epidemic evangelicalism of the mid-eighteenth century, had created challenges to the traditional notions of social stratification by generating the conviction that the ultimate quality of men was to be found elsewhere than in their external condition, and that a cosmic achievement lay within each man's grasp. And the peculiar configuration of colonial politics—a constant broil of petty factions struggling almost formlessly, with little discipline or control, for the benefits of public authority—had tended to erode the respect traditionally accorded the institutions and officers of the state.

Yet nowhere, at any time in the colonial years, were the implications of these circumstances articulated or justified. The assumption remained that society, in its maturity if not in its confused infancy, would conform to the pattern of the past; that authority would continue to exist without challenge, and that those in superior positions would be responsible and wise, and those beneath them respectful and content. These premises and expectations were deeply lodged; they were not easily or quickly displaced. But the Revolution brought with it arguments and attitudes bred of arguments endlessly repeated, that undermined these premises of the *ancien régime.*

For a decade or more defiance to the highest constituted powers poured from the colonial presses and was hurled from half the pulpits of the land. The right, the need, the absolute obligation to disobey legally constituted authority had become the universal cry. Cautions and qualifications became ritualistic: formal exercises in ancient pieties. One might preface one's charge to disobedience with homilies on the inevitable imperfections of all governments and the necessity to bear "some injuries" patiently and peaceably. But what needed and received demonstration and defense was not the caution, but the injunction: the argument that when injuries touched on "fundamental rights" (and who could say when they did not?) then nothing less than "duty to God and religion, to themselves, to the community, and to unborn posterity re-

quire such to assert and defend their rights by all lawful, most prudent, and effectual means in their power." Obedience as a principle was only too well known; disobedience as a doctrine was not. It was therefore asserted again and again that resistance to constituted authority was "a doctrine according to godliness—the doctrine of the English nation . . . by which our rights and constitution have often been defended and repeatedly rescued out of the hands of encroaching tyranny . . . This is the doctrine and grand pillar of the ever memorable and glorious Revolution, and upon which our gracious sovereign George III holds the crown of the British empire." What better credentials could there be? How lame to add that obedience too "is an eminent part of Christian duty without which government must disband and dreadful anarchy and confusion (with all its horrors) take place and reign without control"—how lame, especially in view of the fact that one could easily mistake this "Christian obedience" for that "blind, enslaving obedience which is no part of the Christian institution but is highly injurious to religion, to every free government, and to the good of mankind and is the stirrup of tyranny, and grand engine of slavery." . . .

In such declarations a political argument became a moral imperative. The principle of justifiable disobedience and the instinct to question public authority before accepting it acquired a new sanction and a new vigor. Originally, of course, the doctrine of resistance was applied to Parliament, a non-representative assembly 3,000 miles away. But the composition and location of the institution had not been as crucial in creating opposition as had the character of the actions Parliament had taken. Were provincial assemblies, simply because they were local and representative, exempt from scrutiny and resistance? Were they any less susceptible than Parliament to the rule that when their authority is extended beyond "the bounds of the law of God and the free constitution . . . 'their acts are, *ipso facto,* void, and cannot oblige any to obedience' "? There could be no doubt of the answer. Any legislature, wherever located or however composed, deserved only the obedience it could command by the justice and wisdom of its proceedings. Representative or not, local or not, any agency of the state could be defied. The freeholders of Augusta, Virginia, could not have been more explicit in applying to local government in 1776 the defiance learned in the struggle with Parliament. They wrote their delegates to Virginia's Provincial Congress that

should the future conduct of our legislative body prove to you that our opinion of their wisdom and justice is ill-grounded, then tell them that your constituents are neither guided nor will ever be influenced by that slavish maxim in politics, "that whatever is enacted by that body of men in whom the supreme power of the state is vested must in all cases be obeyed," and that they firmly believe attempts to repeal an unjust law can be vindicated beyond a simple remonstrance addressed to the legislators.

But such threats as these were only the most obvious ways in which traditional notions of authority came into question. Others were more subtly subversive, silently sapping the traditional foundations of social orders and discipline.

"Right" obviously lay at the heart of the Anglo-American controversy: the rights of Englishmen, the rights of mankind, chartered rights. But *"rights,"* wrote Richard Bland—that least egalitarian of Revolutionary leaders—"imply *equality* in the instances to which they belong and must be treated without respect to the dignity of the persons concerned in them." This was by no means simply a worn cliché, for while "equality before the law" was a commonplace of the time, "equality without respect to the dignity of the persons concerned" was not; its emphasis on social equivalence was significant, and though in its immediate context the remark was directed to the invidious distinctions believed to have been drawn between Englishmen and Americans its broader applicability was apparent. Others seized upon it, and developed it, especially in the fluid years of transition when new forms of government were being sought to replace those believed to have proved fatal to liberty. "An affectation of rank" and "the assumed distinction of 'men of consequence' " had been the blight of the Proprietary party, a Pennsylvania pamphleteer wrote in 1776. Riches in a new country like America signified nothing more than the accident of prior settlement. The accumulation of wealth had been "unavoidable to the descendants of the early settlers" since the land, originally cheap, had appreciated naturally with the growth of settlement.

Perhaps it is owing to this accidental manner of becoming rich that wealth does not obtain the same degree of influence here which it does in old countries. Rank, at present, in America is derived more from qualification than property; a sound moral char-

The Ideology of Liberty

acter, amiable manners, and firmness in principle constitute the first class, and will continue to do so till the origin of families be forgotten, and the proud follies of the old world overrun the simplicity of the new.

Therefore, under the new dispensation, "no reflection ought to be made on any man on account of birth, provided that his manners rises decently with his circumstances, and that he affects not to forget the level he came from."

The idea was, in its very nature, corrosive to the traditional authority of magistrates and of established institutions. And it activated other, similar thoughts whose potential threat to stability lay till then inert. There was no more familiar notion in eighteenth-century political thought—it was propounded in every tract on government and every ministerial exhortation to the civil magistracy—than that those who wield power were "servants of society" as well as "ministers of God," and as such had to be specially qualified: they must be acquainted with the affairs of men; they must have wisdom, knowledge, prudence; and they must be men of virtue and true religion. But how far should one go with this idea? The doctrine that the qualifications for magistracy were moral, spiritual, and intellectual could lead to conflict with the expectation that public leaders would be people of external dignity and social superiority; it could be dangerous to the establishment in any settled society. For the ancient notion that leadership must devolve on men whose "personal authority and greatness," whose "eminence or nobility," were such that "every man subordinate is ready to yield a willing submission without contempt or repining"—ordinary people

not easily conceding to an authority "conferred upon a mean man . . . no better than selected out of their own rank"—this traditional notion had never been repudiated, was still honored and repeated. But now, in the heated atmosphere of incipient rebellion, the idea of leaders as servants of the people was pushed to its logical extreme, and its subversive potentialities revealed. By 1774 it followed from the belief that "lawful rulers are the servants of the people" that they were "exalted above their brethren not for their own sakes, but for the benefit of the people; and submission is yielded, not on account of their persons considered exclusively on the authority they are clothed with, but of those laws which in the exercise of this authority are made by them conformably to the laws of nature and equity." In the distribution of offices, it was said in 1770, "merit only in the candidate" should count—not birth, or wealth, or loyalty to the great; but merit only. Even a deliberately judicious statement of this theme rang with defiance to traditional forms of authority: "It is not wealth—it is not family—it is not either of these alone, nor both of them together, though I readily allow neither is to be disregarded, that will qualify men for important seats in government, unless they are rich and honorable in other and more important respects." Indeed, one could make a complete inversion and claim that, properly, the external affluence of magistrates should be the consequence of, not the prior qualification for, the judicious exercise of public authority over others. . . .

By 1774 it seemed undeniable to many, uninvolved in or hostile to the

Revolutionary effort, that declarations "before GOD . . . that it is no rebellion to oppose any king, ministry, or governor [who] destroys by any violence or authority whatever the rights of the people" threatened the most elemental principles of order and discipline in society. . . .

Their fears were in a sense justified, for in the context of eighteenth-century social thought it was difficult to see how any harmonious, stable social order could be constructed from such materials. To argue that all men were equal would not make them so; it would only help justify and perpetuate that spirit of defiance, that refusal to concede to authority whose ultimate resolution could only be anarchy, demagoguery, and tyranny. If such ideas prevailed year after year, generation after generation, the "latent spark" in the breasts of even the most humble of men would be kindled again and again by entrepreneurs of discontent who would remind the people "of the elevated rank they hold in the universe, as men; that all men by nature are equal; that kings are but the ministers of the people; that their authority is delegated to them by the people for their good, and they have a right to resume it, and place it in other hands, or keep it themselves, whenever it is made use of to oppress them." Seeds of sedition would thus constantly be sown, and harvests of licentiousness reaped.

How else could it end? What reasonable social and political order could conceivably be built and maintained where authority was questioned before it was obeyed, where social differences were considered to be incidental rather than essential to community order, and where superiority, suspect in principle, was not allowed to concentrate in the hands of a few but was scattered broadly through the populace? No one could clearly say. But some, caught up in a vision of the future in which the peculiarities of American life became the marks of a chosen people, found in the defiance of traditional order the firmest of all grounds for their hope for a freer life. The details of this new world were not as yet clearly depicted; but faith ran high that a better world than any that had ever been known could be built where authority was distrusted and held in constant scrutiny; where the status of men flowed from their achievements and from their personal qualities, not from distinction ascribed to them at birth; and where the use of power over lives of men was jealously guarded and severely restricted. It was only where there was this defiance, this refusal to truckle, this distrust of all authority, political or social, that institutions would express human aspirations, not crush them.

For JAMES KIRBY MARTIN (b. 1943), the impact of the Revolution on the people can best be understood only after the needs, expectations, and frustrations of the principal insurgent actors have been explored. In *Men in Rebellion: Higher Government Leaders and the Coming of the American Revolution*, he emphasizes that tensions pointing toward the Revolution arose as much from a structural crisis in the distribution of power and political offices in the provinces as from other issue-related factors. The rebellion unfolded as a crisis within the political elite and ultimately saw insurgent lesser officials overthrow British authority and replace it with systems of government that allowed men like themselves to maximize their opportunities for advancement on an open and competitive basis. In so doing, they opened the door, however slightly, to the possibility of popular reform for all the people in the years ahead.

# A Formative Crisis Within the Elite

Patterns of behavior among officeholders in the political arena tend to reflect their positions within the structure of political systems. Political structures normally are hierarchical; offices on higher levels by function usually have a broader range of authority, and they command greater prestige and respect than do offices on lower levels. By definition, then, offices on higher levels are fewer in number, making it impossible for all office seekers to attain them. Individuals making the decision to enter politics characteristically, though not always, begin political careers by fulfilling the responsibilities of lower-level offices. They perceive politics from that vantage point, but they hope to work their way up through the hierarchy so as to gain greater status and authority associated with higher-level offices. As mobility occurs, moreover, perceptions of responsibilities and political reality

From James Kirby Martin, *Men in Rebellion: Higher Governmental Leaders and the Coming of the American Revolution* (New Brunswick, 1973), pp. 23-26, 173-183, 189-192. Reprinted by permission of the Rutgers University Press. Footnotes omitted.

change. Ultimately few succeed in their drive to balance expectations with achievements, and levels of expectation do vary from person to person. Yet as long as fluidity in the form of mobility (opportunity for personal and group political advancement) denotes the system, both those who succeed and those who fail retain the sense that the system has some merit and should not be seriously modified except by chance, fortune, or political necessity through time.

That some men should quest for political power is a normal part of the political process. The quest continues every day and gives momentum to political change and the rise and decline of political movements. Structurally, the process of officeholder interaction does not usually get out of hand and lead to coups, palace rebellions, and broader peoples' revolutions unless individuals seeking positions of greater power and prominence metamorphose into groups which feel that opportunity for advancement and upward political mobility is too narrowly confined, or worse yet, nonexistent. The "outs," collecting in lower-level offices and finding both security and unity in numbers, have two real alternatives open to them. They may aggrandize as much authority as possible at the highest level to which they may advance in the political structure, normally accomplished by cutting into the powers and prerogatives of higher officials. Or they may speak out against the right of the higher "in" group to rule. If those dominating at higher levels remain insensitive to "out" group pressures, do not find new avenues of mobility, or attempt to reassert lost authority, then they may very well

precipitate rebellion. Clearly, the first pattern of "out" group response characterized colonial American politics after 1689, from the time of the Gloriour Revolution in America to the end of the Seven Years' War in 1763. But after that date, the second pattern of response (potential rebellion) became the new mark of late colonial political reality.

The hypothesis here is that political immobility caused stress in the colonial political systems and underlay much of the tensions giving motion to the developing American Revolution. Out factions had coalesced in one form or another in all of the colonies prior to 1763; they were devoted to circumscribing the prerogatives of higher royal officials in the provincial political structure. Such factions, coming together in lower houses of Assemblies, began to consider the possibility of rebellion after 1763 when reinvigorated imperial programs proscribed many of the prerogatives assemblymen had won. Thus the "out" factions, sensing a relative loss of power and seeing no alternative avenues for political mobility, faced the bleak prospect of losing what had been gained or forcing the system open through rebellion. The latter course was the only viable alternative for lower-level officials collectively frustrated by political immobility.

Before proceeding further, however, definitions are in order. If we define the prerevolutionary *political elite* as all those individuals who held political offices, whether on local, county, or colony-wide levels in the provincial political structures, then definite patterns emerge more clearly from the data. Tensions were building between "lesser" and "higher" officials causing increasing amounts of political insta- bility and disequilibrium as the 1760s and 1770s unfolded. Lesser officials here are defined as those leaders carry- ing out the duties attached to local and county offices as well as legislators in the lower houses of the thirteen colon- ial Assemblies. In the years immediate- ly prior to the disruption of colonial governments, many of them were at one and the same time political *in- cumbents* and political *insurgents*. Such men were a major part of the late colonial political elite, but they were lesser officials theoretically subordi- nate to royal authority in that elite. Higher officials, on the other hand, were those favored few men who clustered around royal and proprietary governors. They were men in colony- wide offices above the Assembly level, men who normally gained their posi- tions through appointive procedures and who represented the presumed monarchical and aristocratic social orders in government. The term "high- er," derived from the eighteenth- century hierarchical conception of mixed government, is here specifically applied to those executive leaders under study. Prerevolutionary higher- level officeholders were a small but not insignificant number, given the re- assertion of imperial authority after 1763, in the late colonial political elite.

Tensions among lesser and higher officials were manifest well before the decades of revolution. Political incum- bents on the Assembly level and be- low often formed "country" or "whig" factions in their thrust toward ex- panding the powers and prerogatives of lower houses vis-à-vis royal and proprietary governors and councilors. Higher officials, on the other hand, usually congregated into "court" or "tory" factions in defensive reaction. Experiencing little or no support from uninterested and lackadaisical Crown officials in England until the 1760s, higher officials fought a losing battle to preserve and protect the prerogatives of royal and proprietary governments. Leaders in the lower houses persisted in their attempts to aggrandize author- ity, and the clash of factions resulted. Who would control financial matters and the distribution of tax monies? Would governors or Assembly leaders have the final authority to determine speakers of the house? Would gover- nors or assemblymen have the power to decide what developing frontier regions would be represented in As- semblies? Would royal officials in the colonies be dependent upon Assem- blies for salaries? Who would control Indian policies? The attempt to re- solve such questions set the tone of factional disputes, at least until the early 1760s when home officials began to reassert royal authority through the implementation of more rigorous im- perial programs. Then the nature, the quality, and the content of factional bickering changed.

Though setting the tone of eighteenth- century politics, factionalism in itself does not have the power to explain the dynamics of the coming Revolu- tion. We must ask what factors served to shape factional lines and ultimately to make political reconciliation impos- sible. Remembering that offices and individual political careers were as much at stake as were royal and pro- prietary prerogatives, we may say that political immobility was both a *pre- condition* of party factionalism as well as a *precipitant* of revolution once

British policy changed course after the Seven Years' War. We must now investigate why lesser officials found themselves frustrated by advancement procedures prior to the outbreak of fighting revolution. . . .

The grand question facing political activists at any point in time is that of who should rule on what level of the political structure. The failure to resolve that question set the stage for the outbreak of the American Revolution. American community leaders, able to aspire to seats in lower houses of Assemblies, insisted upon Assembly autonomy in internal political matters. By 1763 legislators held the balance of power in decision-making. Yet after nearly a century of ministerial indifference about the increasing authority of lower houses, Parliament began to approve new imperial programs following the Seven Years' War and the de facto autonomy that community socioeconomic leaders had acquired as assemblymen. Lesser officials in lower houses refused to concede prerogatives. With no prospect for political mobility above the Assembly level, many of them saw no reason to hand back what they had taken from their opponents in higher offices. Instead, community leaders reacted to political tensions and personal frustrations by depersonalizing the problem and issuing statements to the effect that British appointees in the provinces were partakers in a ministerial conspiracy to destroy American liberties. Higher officials became noxious tools in the plot. They were agents of the ministry and corrupted by the lure of official favor and high office. They were about to corrupt in turn the known liberties of all provincial citizens.

Higher officials had been losing the factional contest over prerogatives and authority for many years. No doubt they were willing to regain lost powers. But implementation of imperial plans was no easy task. Whether higher officials liked it or not, they had to attempt to make imperial programs work, that is if they wanted to keep their offices and the respect that they felt was due them as men of high official standing. Some of them as a result became the selected victims of group protest and intimidation; roving mobs of irate colonists destroyed their property and prized personal possessions. An even greater number of executives felt the barbed sting of insurgent charges about corruption. They became the most hated men in the provinces. When the Crown and Parliament in the early 1770s finally refused to concede the American position, higher officials found themselves not only the victims of insurgent words but also of growing rebellion. Tensions, hatred, and frustrations boiled over into irreconciliation; political consensus about the importance of British sovereignty gave way to armed conflict. A power vacuum developed as governments collapsed. American community leaders, many of whom had gained years of political experience as lesser officials, took charge of the revolutionary cause.

The power vacuum did not last long. The end of British and the beginning of popular sovereignty came through the state constitutions of 1776 and 1777. Many of the lesser officials and future revolutionary leaders studied here (62.3 per cent) attended one or more of the provincial congresses which capped resistance to imperial authority by producing new constitutional frameworks for state governments. A new political environment emerged out of the destruction of royal authority in America.

The men who wrote the new constitutions, if at all typical of those participants under investigation here, had needs and expectations which they hoped would be realized in the revolutionary political arena. Many no doubt sought political preferment in high offices. After all, the men who became revolutionary executives were not politically inexperienced, but they had been active as lesser officials before the Revolution. Given the frustrations as well as the expectations of such men, the hypothesis is that insurgent leaders purged their political frustrations by writing constitutions which permitted men like themselves, men of community socioeconomic accomplishments, to compete for high offices. The new constitutions became the vehicles through which political immobility ceased to be an irritating phenomenon for those not favored by Crown procedures of advancement before the Revolution.

This is not to say that political theory had no meaning or importance to the constitution-makers. There is overwhelming evidence that leaders in constitutional conventions had read widely in ancient and modern political treatises. Yet men also came to the conventions with a lifetime of experiences and specific personal goals. Many such men wanted and took high offices when the opportunity presented itself in 1776 and 1777. The experiential dimension must not be neglected for those who wrote constitutions and desired high office. Their political expectations were about to become achievements.

There was both uniformity and variety in the theoretical foundations of the state constitutions. Many leaders spoke and thought in terms of "republicanism"; citizens had to be virtuous; governments could be effective and stable only if the commonalty did not abuse the public trust for immediate personal gain. Yet within the context of republicanism there was no consistent pattern in relocating the balance among the three traditional orders in government. There was no rush to level the orders and to put all power in the hands of common citizens, despite expressions of popular sovereignty. On one side the Pennsylvania constitution-makers were least concerned with preserving balance. The first state constitution collapsed the traditional orders into one by eliminating the chief executive and by placing legislative authority in a popularly elected unicameral Assembly. Virtuous Pennsylvanians won the right to rule themselves through their annually elected representatives without upper-hierarchy restraints. But Pennsylvania was not typical; it was a real experiment in republicanism. The constitutional environments created in several other states emphasized hierarchical balance and placed checks upon the democracy of citizens. In Maryland, one of the most restrictive constitutions, the leaders (men of planter and commercial wealth) retained a sense of balance by approving among other provisions high property-holding qualifications for those in high offices. The presumption was that governors or state senators with substantial personal wealth would be less tempted by the possible corruptions of office; they would be less likely to ignore public needs for petty personal interests; they would be more willing to stand against unreasonable popular pressures from below and potential democratic excesses in decision-making.

Few of the delegates to the constitutional conventions were social or political levelers. They were men of community standing. They believed in order and balance. They did not doubt their own talents or proven character, but they were not committed to the notion that common citizens had the ability to rule themselves in intelligence and wisdom. Yet they were willing, as a second hypothesis, to expand the political rights of common citizens in the political arena so as to guarantee that men like themselves would have open access to offices on all levels of government. Cautiously making popular sovereignty something more than a hollow phrase, this extension of political rights proved to be a major step forward toward the decline of deferential politics in the eighteenth century.

To gain political hegemony as well as to end the pattern of political immobility, insurgent leaders employed several constitutional devices. First of all they saw to it that executive offices which formerly had been appointive became either directly or indirectly elective. Delegates adopted a variety of procedures to insure that the diffusion of the power to appoint shifted downward into the hands of voting citizens or their elected representatives in lower and upper houses of Assemblies. The norm was to grant enfranchised voters the right to elect state senators (formerly Crown-appointed councilors). Elected assemblymen and senators, meeting in state capitals, would fill other executive offices through joint balloting of both houses. Indeed, there was no more striking way to break apart the control that a handful of Crown and proprietary officials had exercised over executive appointments. There was no more potent means to assure that community socioeconomic leaders would have the opportunity to compete for high offices. Now voting citizens (white adult men who long had been accustomed within the deferential framework to electing local men of standing to community offices and to lower houses of Assemblies) rather than distant British officials would determine which prominent local elite gentleman would serve in elective high offices. Community leaders then would gather in Assemblies and determine what other men of ability, talent, and merit would carry out the duties of the remaining offices.

There were few exceptions to the new provisions for the selection of higher officials. Joint balloting of both houses usually extended to secretaries and attorneys general, and in fewer cases to supreme court judges. In New Jersey, Delaware, Virginia, North Carolina, lower and upper houses voted each year to fill governorships. In Delaware the president (governor) met with the houses of Assembly to name supreme court judges; the president with the advice of his privy council selected the secretary and attorney general. New York was an exception in another direction because the constitution-makers provided for direct, popular election of the governor and lieutenant governor. The New Yorkers also established a council of appointment, made up of four senators and the governor, who were to name all other nonelective officers in government, that is with the exception of the treasurer. The lower house had the prerogative to appoint the treasurer, since all financial matters were to originate in and be controlled by that body.

The only state constitution that modified the emerging pattern of direct election of senators was Maryland. There the upper-class citizens who controlled the convention consciously kept the election of state senators one step removed from popular ratification. The enfranchised voters in the state would ballot on election day for electors who in turn would gather at Annapolis to pick state senators, chosen either from their own number or from the general population. Given property-holding qualifications for senators, Maryland constitution-makers sought to guarantee that men of wealth (proven ability or high birth) would check leveling influences rising from the lower house.

In conjunction with the direct or indirect election of higher officials, the constitution-makers, second, shattered the old appointive mechanism by establishing fixed election districts for offices not statewide in scope and authority. Indeed, representation based upon population distribution had its first application in some revolutionary governments. State senators were to be chosen from specific geographic districts, thereby presenting at least in name definite constituencies in the body politic. New Hampshire assigned each county councilors (senators) according to the number of residents in the county. This provision actually infuriated citizens in the more remote

and less populous western Connecticut Valley region. Western community leaders understood that easterners would dominate in actual numbers in the Assembly. They knew that equity in legislation and governmental appropriations would not be their lot. Proportional representation in New Hampshire became one argument to stir a western secessionist movement occurring before the War for Independence had ended. New Yorkers avoided upstate ire by establishing a septennial census, to commence after the war. First, the constitution-makers sectioned off four senatorial election districts; each district had a quota of senators according to the number of freeholders in the respective district. If census-takers found at the end of seven years that population shifts had taken place, then a redistribution of seats was to follow. That way southern and eastern areas would be unable to retain a disproportionate share of senators as population spread north and west. If the census-takers discovered, moreover, that freeholders in any district had increased relative to all electors in the state by one twenty-fourth, then the senatorial district would get an additional seat. New York planned to expand the number of senators as population grew, but Virginia constitution-makers did not take future population shifts into consideration in mapping out twenty-four senatorial districts. The eastern planters in the convention thus guaranteed that they would have more senatorial power than their constituent numbers deserved, since population already was building in the west. North Carolinians, by comparison, assigned each county a senator regardless of population. Western settlements were favored and would continue to be as new counties were set off, counties which were unlikely at first to have the same number of freeholders as those in the east.

No matter what the constitutional device and what part of the population (eastern or western) favored, the impact of spreading out senatorial election districts was profound in terms of changing leadership patterns. Landholding, professional, and mercantile families of great wealth and imperial standing tended to congregate in or near cultural and economic centers like Boston, New York, or Philadelphia, or they had convenient access to colonial capitals such as Williamsburg or Annapolis. Developing western regions, on the other hand, rarely produced individuals before 1774 with enough earned family status and personal wealth to gain the attention of royal governors living among leaders of the great families in eastern urban centers and capitals. Thus the better sort from coastal regions and cities were in a most favorable competitive position for high offices; they proved to be a major source of executive appointees.

But effective great family monopolization could not continue with election districts located all over the states, with the diffusion of the appointive power downward into the hands of voters and elected leaders in lower and upper houses, and with residency requirements placed on elective offices. As a third safeguard to the insurgents' interest, several of the state constitutions made it mandatory for senatorial candidates to live, not just own property, in election districts. Actual inhabitants were to represent constitu-

ents. Thus families with extensive kinship connections, even if present in several communities, were unlikely to have relatives with residences in enough districts so that domination of executive offices could continue. Even in those areas where great families lived, they now had to compete for high offices at the polls with men of somewhat lesser stature, but nonetheless community leaders. The data suggest that the importance of family ties declined with the invocation of new governments. Diffusion of the appointive power and fixed election districts along with residency requirements broke the hold that many eastern families of distinction exercised over high offices while at the same time strengthening the competitive position of local community leaders everywhere.

The constitution-makers, fourth, attacked privileged control and political immobility by setting tenure restrictions upon executive offices. Unchecked tenure had been one major source of immobility before the Revolution. But after 1776 there were few cases where the incumbent might presume that there would be no challenge to his authority. The governors of New Jersey, Delaware, Virginia, North Carolina, and South Carolina had to face joint balloting and the threat of expulsion from office each year. The popularly elected upper houses of New Hampshire, New Jersey, and North Carolina were to be contested at the polls annually. Delaware chose a three-year term of office for state senators; New York and Virginia, wanting more stability, agreed upon four-year terms. Maryland again demonstrated its upperclass conservatism by placing senators under five-year terms of office. In those executive positions in which joint balloting determined the incumbent, terms of office varied but were normally longer than elective positions. Judges of the New Jersey supreme court had seven years; the attorney general and secretary five; the treasurer but one year. Delaware decided that the secretary and attorney general should hold office for five years yet permitted supreme court judges to serve during "good behavior," the norm for judicial tenure in some states. New York supreme court judges, in a novel provision, were to have office during good behavior or until they reached a mandatory retirement age of sixty.

Such limitations had two definite effects upon leadership change and prospects for political mobility. First, tenure checks made it more difficult to hold offices indefinitely. Second, it became possible for prospective candidates from among local leadership ranks to challenge officeholders periodically and even to gain offices for themselves without having to wait an inordinantly long number of years. The first observation is borne out in the data about the number of years that late colonial (open-ended tenure) and revolutionary executives (closed-ended tenure) were in office. The first group averaged 10.7 years before the Revolution cut them short while the second group averaged 5.9 years before other challengers stepped into their positions. The very fact that revolutionary executives held office for briefer terms establishes the second point that more men had greater opportunity to experience political mobility after 1776.

Not only did the constitution-makers place checks on tenure by assigning definite terms to offices, but in a few notable instances they also went so far as to adopt the principle of "rotation of office." Both the Virginia and Maryland governors, for example, were not to serve any more than three years in succession out of seven. The same provision applied to supreme executive councilors in Pennsylvania. According to constitution-makers there, rotation stopped "the danger of establishing an inconvenient aristrocracy" while it also meant that "more men will be trained to public business." As David Ramsay stated, "The favorers of this system of rotation contended for it, as likely to prevent a perpetuity of office and power in the same individual or family, and as a security against hereditary honors."

The constitution-makers, finally, sanctioned a variety of provisions directed against plural officeholding. But there was no pattern to the procedures. Supreme court judges in New York were not permitted to hold any other office, except that of delegate to the Continental Congress. The treasurer and attorney general of Pennsylvania were not to sit consecutively in the Assembly or the supreme executive council. Senators and assemblymen in Maryland and South Carolina could not at the same time hold salaried offices, but the South Carolinians could accept officers' commissions in local or Continental military units. Treasurers in North Carolina were barred from the house and senate until they had settled all accounts with the state. Many such clauses arose from the desires of constitution-makers to avoid conflicting interests among men in office, but the provisions likewise made it illegal for one man to acquire more than his share of executive offices.

More men could compete for more offices.

Thus several constitutional procedures worked to the advantage of those lesser officials desiring the opportunity to hold high offices before 1774. Yet at the same time a strange paradox grew out of constitution-making, directly affecting those insurgents who became executives in 1776 and 1777. We may discern the paradox by looking at two dimensions of state constitution-making rather than just one. On one dimension provisions made mobility possible for rising community leaders. Yet on an equally important dimension, the new constitutions put several checks upon the prerogatives that revolutionary higher officials were to exercise while in office. Governors were hardest hit. Many of them lost the right to veto legislation, to make political appointments, to adjourn, prorogue, and dissolve self-willed Assemblies. New Hampshire and Pennsylvania went so far as to eliminate the governor altogether from politics. Many upper houses lost the ability to influence the nature and the scope of money bills. The new constitutions located more prerogatives and powers in lower houses than ever had been the de facto case under British sovereignty. These two dimensions in constitution-making thus converged at a point where insurgent lesser officials moved into executive offices when the authority of lower houses was reaching a new zenith. Insurgents gained access to offices which had fewer powers attached to them than at any previous time in the century.

What caused the confusion in the efforts of the constitution-makers? Why would they work to open the door to executive offices while stripping many of these same positions of powers? Why would lesser officials rush to fill these offices, apparently weaker in range of authority, in 1776 and 1777? The answer to these questions lies in the nature of the insurgent quest for power and political preferment before the outbreak of revolution. Community socioeconomic leaders found through experience that British advancement procedures did not favor men with their qualifications. Leaders in lower houses, then, congregated into factions and used their political energy to cut into the prerogatives of higher officeholders frustrating their political ambitions. The incessant factional duel over prerogatives reflected the desires of lesser officials to consolidate as much authority as possible on the level of officeholding (lower houses) that was within their range of acquisition. Even though Assembly leaders slashed deeply into Crown and proprietary territory, their victory was never complete, and reverses were setting in with Crown support after 1763. Even in the years of collapsing imperial authority, governors and other court faction leaders had the ability to stymie local legislative wants. Governors still had the veto power and the right to adjourn, prorogue, and dissolve Assemblies. When the factional contest finally undermined all respect for imperial authority, constitution-makers resolved the contest by putting the brunt of decision-making prerogatives in the lower houses, the base of prerevolutionary insurgent operations. It was the logical culmination of the whig "quest for power" in the absence of restraining imperial authority.

Constitution-makers, nonetheless,

were aware of the need to promote political mobility for community socioeconomic leaders. Political preferment remained the deferred aspect of the insurgent quest; frustrations about political advancement had been a precondition to the solidification of factional lines on a vertical plane dictating the drive against the prerogatives of upper-hierarchy appointive officials before 1774. Hence the constitution-makers also responded to the needs of men for access to high office. Community leaders, most certainly aware of the circumscribed authority of high offices, did not hesitate but rushed into the void in executive leadership. These positions, moreover, still had some powers, and being the most visible offices, were prestigious, adding greatly to the status of known community leaders of talent and merit. Denied high offices before the Revolution, the first constitutional settlement denied lesser officials some authority once in high office. It would take time and further constitutional settlements before the imbalance would redress itself. . . .

One revolutionary Virginian visiting Williamsburg in November 1776 commented that he had taken "a view of our new Assembly, now sitting—under the happy auspices of the People only." He described the scene in vivid fashion:

I confess I am pleased—and though it is composed of men not quite so well dressed, nor so politely educated, nor so highly born as some Assemblies I have formerly seen—yet upon the whole I like their Proceedings—and upon the whole rather better than formerly. They are the People's men (and the People in general are right). They are plain and of consequence less disguised, but I believe to be full as honest, less intriguing, more sincere.

The Virginian did not feel detachment but a new sense of involvement in government and the process of political decision-making. He did not write deferentially but almost scornfully about upper-class gentlemen. He betrayed a faith that the people knew their needs best, and he thought the people were in control of Virginia's government. His comments about the emerging political order were premature, if not overly optimistic.

A new political order was developing, no doubt, but not necessarily because of popular upheaval and the appearance of common men in high political office. The question of who should rule at home had been vital to the process making for revolution, as Carl Becker described it so ably many years ago, but the nature of the internal crisis was not so much a contest between the masses and the upper classes. It was not so much a direct, internal confrontation between those few with great wealth and the vast majority of citizens with little or no property. Neither did the Revolution solely gain momentum, as Robert E. Brown suggested, from the desires of middle-class men to preserve and sustain a democratic order. Indeed, leadership analysis tends to the conclusion that the confrontation after 1763 resulted not so much from a class struggle as from a struggle within the ruling class, if we may apply those terms to the lesser and higher officials making up the late colonial political elite. Were community socioeconomic leaders to control the destiny of American politics and to have open access to all, not just some, offices in government? Or were a few nonnative placemen and privileged native gentlemen of wealth, education, family standing, and imperial connections to dominate in high offices and frustrate community leaders by their presence and their willingness to carry through on imperial programs? Were lesser officials to have autonomy in political matters, or were higher officials (dependent upon Crown patronage) to corrupt American liberties because of their lust for power and preferment? More specifically, was it to be Patrick Henry or Lord Dunmore in the governorship of Virginia? Was William Henry Drayton to be denied a judgeship on the South Carolina circuit court? Were the Otises to be frustrated in their family political ambitions in Massachusetts by the better-placed Hutchinsons and Olivers? American community leaders, in the end, unwilling to accept imperial plans and all that such programs implied about subordination to royal authority and higher officials, resolved all such questions resoundingly in their favor.

This is not meant to imply that common citizens were wholly passive agents in the process of revolution. Citizens protested, imbibed phrases like "no taxation without representation," formed mobs, and struck out in selective fashion against imperial-oriented officials in government. But mobs are not always class conscious and solely made up of poor and desperate individuals. Mobs have organizers and leaders who determine targets and specify the goals in the coercion of people and destruction of property. Organizers of mobs after 1763 often were those lesser officials and whig faction leaders in government who were contesting with higher officials attempting to do the will of Parliament. The crowd was a means to an end; it was brute force

with the power of intimidation and destruction to be used when men could not get what they wanted through the normal channels of politics. In the end common citizens, those who participated in mob activity and those who remained silent, benefited from the insurgent drive against higher officials. Their reward for supporting the insurgents was broader participation in the revolutionary political arena.

Thus common citizens became involved, but they rarely led. The weight of their numbers made whig threats and entreaties against imperial politics and higher officials all that more forceful. Citizens lent strength, but the preconditions and precipitants of revolution grew out of the frustrations of insurgent community leaders. The American Revolution from the outset was a contest for power involving men in power.

And the weight of popular support was the trump card of insurgent leaders. Royal and proprietary authorities lacked numbers in their collection of resources. They depended far too much upon lackadaisical ministries and popular consensus about the advantages of British sovereignty. Indeed, when Crown officials tried to balance off the void in numbers through the counterforce of red-coated British regular troops, they only further aggravated tensions and made the whig appeal about conspiracy and loss of liberties more vividly real. One need only think of the ineffectiveness of British regiments sent to Boston in the late summer of 1768 to quell popular disturbances directed against Crown officials. Confrontation of significant proportions eventually came in the Boston Massacre of March 1770, and a greater victory could not have been had for insurgent leaders. British troops, no matter who was at fault, now were killing *Americans* on *American* soil. British troops as a counterforce to the popular numbers backing whig insurgents abetted rather than deterred attitudes of American community solidarity and identity.

Royal and proprietary officials were losing control, moreover, because they failed to perceive that the unity of whig factions had some potential to be broken by the promotion of some lesser officials with fewer imperial credentials into higher offices. Would the sequence of events in Massachusetts have been different had James Otis, Sr., become the chief justice in 1760? Was the problem that court faction leaders were so hungry for their own political preferment that they could not perceive the need to keep political systems fluid and to provide opportunities for community leaders of merit who were lesser officials to move up the political hierarchy of offices? Would insurgent leaders have responded to such offers after the pull of the current of rebellion became so strong and have agreed to political elevation for themselves rather than destroying the political system sustaining so many Wentworths, Hutchinsons, Olivers, De Lanceys, Penns, Carters, and Bulls in higher offices? Such questions are speculative and based upon hindsight. Yet they point to a flaw, a blind spot in the counterstrategy of British officials, a failure to understand that systems lacking in mobility for qualified candidates have the potential to be disrupted through open rebellion. That failure of vision on the part of British officials abetted the destruction of the Anglo-American empire.

LINDA GRANT DE PAUW (b. 1940) has concluded
that the consequences of the Revolution were hardly
revolutionary for the bulk of the people. In her essay,
"Land of the Unfree," De Pauw argues that despite
the rhetoric, the ideals, and the actions of those who
opposed Great Britain, the historical record indicates
that not more than 15 percent of the Revolutionary
generation was actually in a position to enjoy promises
of life, liberty, and happiness more fully. As many
second-class citizens fell outside the pale of "liberty"
and "freedom for all" after the decades of the
Revolution as before. If the bulk of the people were
unable to increase their personal rights through the
Revolution, then what was the Revolution all about?
Can her arguments be reconciled with those of
Jameson, Bailyn, and Martin to form an interpretation
of the role of the people?

# *Land of the Unfree:*
# *Legal Limitations on Liberty*
# *in Revolutionary America*

The fortune that Thomas Jefferson
pledged with his life and sacred honor
in support of the declaration that all
men are created equal and endowed
with inalienable rights to life, liberty,
and the pursuit of happiness, included,
in the summer of 1776, almost two
hundred slaves. The incongruity of a
slave-owning people basing their Revolution on such exalted doctrines did
not escape remark by contemporaries
any more than it has escaped notice
by historians. "How is it" sneered
Samuel Johnson, "that we hear the
loudest *yelps* for liberty among the
drivers of negroes?" The Loyalist
Thomas Hutchinson dryly observed
that there seemed to be some dis-
crepancy between the declaration that
all men were equal and a practice that
deprived "more than a hundred thousand Africans of their rights to liberty."
Even those Englishmen who sym-
pathized with the American cause were

From Linda Grant De Pauw, "Land of the Unfree: Legal Limitations on Liberty in
Pre-Revolutionary America," *Maryland Historical Magazine*, LXVIII (1973), pp. 355–368.
Reprinted by permission of the Maryland Historical Society and the author. Footnotes
omitted.

repelled by the paradox. "If there be an object truly ridiculous in nature," Thomas Day commented, "it is an American patriot signing resolutions of independence with the one hand, and with the other brandishing a whip over his affrighted slaves." And the patriots themselves were not insensitive to it. "I have sometimes been ready to think," Abigail Adams wrote to her husband, "that the passion for liberty cannot be equally strong in the breasts of those who have been accustomed to deprive their fellow creatures of theirs." Patrick Henry confessed amazement that men as sincerely "fond of liberty" and genuinely religious as himself tolerated slavery. "Would anyone believe," he asked "I am the master of slaves of my own purchase!"

Historians writing about the age of the American Revolution have tended to ignore the paradox more frequently than they have attempted to resolve it, but in recent years serious attention has been given to the enslaved blacks, and such New Left historians as Jesse Lemish and Staughton Lynd have pointed out the limitations on the rights of such groups as merchant seamen and urban workers. Yet the full magnitude of the paradox is still unmeasured, for it appears that the contradiction between Lockean ideals and social practice in the year 1776 was not only more pronounced than contemporaries and traditional historians described but even exceeds the dimensions suggested by recent historians of the New Left. Had Lockean dicta been applied to all the human beings in British North America on the eve of the Revolution, and had all been permitted to enjoy the natural and legal rights of freemen, it would have been necessary to alter the status of more than 85 percent of the population. In law and in fact no more than 15 percent of the Revolutionary generation was free to enjoy life, liberty, and the pursuit of happiness unhampered by any restraints except those to which they had given their consent.

The unfree of Revolutionary America may be conveniently considered in five categories: Negroes, white servants, women, minors, and propertyless adult white males. These categories overlap and the proportion of the total population falling into each of the categories differed from one part of the country to another. Thus there were proportionately more women in New England than in backcountry North Carolina, many more blacks, proportionately, in Virginia than in New Jersey, and a larger proportion of disfranchised adult white males in South Carolina than in Massachusetts.

It is also true that legal limitations on liberty do not necessarily coincide either with a psychological sense of freedom or with social practices. The unfree were rarely, in fact, exploited to the full limit allowed by law. Nor has there been any attempt in this brief essay to present a precise description of legal status based on the myriad of local traditions, statutes, and common law interpretation. The following summaries claim to be correct in outline, not to have exhausted the complexities of the subject which are vast and largely unstudied. It is clear, however, that for each of the unfree groups the law placed definite theoretical limits on the rights Locke viewed as inalienable.

The black slaves, the most visible of the colonial unfree, comprised approximately 20 percent of the colonial population, a proportion twice as great as that formed by the black population of the United States today. These slaves were legally chattel property. The law saw no self-evident right to liberty attached to the person of the dark-skinned laborer from Africa, and, indeed, the law had little concern for his right to life. The deliberate murder of a slave was not necessarily a felony in Virginia before the Revolution, for the law assumed that no one would intentionally destroy his own estate. Slaves had no right to hold property of their own and enjoyed the use of no more than the master allowed. As for the third right in Jefferson's trinity, pursuing happiness, if that took the form of taking time off from the master's work, it was a punishable offense.

There were a small number of free blacks in Revolutionary America, most of them in the North. Their status was superior to that of the slave, but they were still limited politically, socially, and economically in all of the colonies. For most legal purposes there was no distinction made between free and enslaved Negroes. They might have some time they could call their own for pursuing happiness, but they were forbidden to pursue it in a tavern. In Rhode Island a free black man could not even purchase a quart of cider.

White servants in colonial America comprised a class perhaps half as large as the slave force but unbalanced in age and sex distribution in favor of young adult males. Their status was superior to that of Negroes but still substantially below that of freemen. In many ways the servant was merely a slave with prospects of eventual free-

dom and whose entry into his lowly station had been more or less voluntary. When, in November 1775, Lord Dunmore attempted to lure blacks into the British army by offering them freedom as a bounty, the same offer was extended to white servants.

The servant's labor belonged to his master twenty-four hours a day, seven days a week. Like the black slave, he was a chattel. He had no property himself but what his master allowed. He could not marry without his master's permission and, like a black man, he could not drink liquor in a tavern. Running away and disobedience were severely punished, and stories of inhuman cruelty to white servants are common. Like a slave, a white servant could be sold against his will away from his wife and family or seized to satisfy his master's debts. There seems little to recommend the legislation governing servants over that governing blacks—with one exception. White servants, unlike slaves, had personal rights to life and contract rights to a minimum standard of living. They could bring suit to enforce these rights and the courts would enforce them even to the extent of freeing the servant outright.

The legal status of colonial women was determined by the tradition of the British common law with certain modifications forced by pioneer American conditions, most of which were made before the end of the seventeenth century. Blackstone's *Commentaries,* which began to circulate as an admired authority among colonial lawyers in the decade before the Revolution, described a theoretical position for English females that varied substantially from that held by free English men.

Under common law, Blackstone taught, a woman ceased to exist if she married, for she and her spouse became one flesh and the flesh was his. She was no longer responsible for her debts or even for all of her personal actions. She had no legal control over any property either inherited or earned. And if her husband judged her disobedient or saucy he could chastise her as he did his children and servants. This was considered proper as he might be held responsible for her misbehaviour in cases short of murder and high treason. Although divorce laws were relatively liberal for a time in the seventeenth century, a reaction in the Revolutionary era made divorce, regardless of cause, practically impossible for a woman to obtain.

The status of unmarried women, both widows and spinsters, was considerably better. By a law of 1419 known as "couverte de Baron" an unattached woman, the "Feme Sole," was entitled to engage in business enterprises on her own account. A widow was entitled to one-third of the family estate and might be willed even more. So long as she did not remarry she could invest or dispose of this property as she wished. There was, however, great social pressure on women to marry. Although women made up almost half of the total population when all age groups are included, the sex ratio of men to women in the marriageable age group (i.e., between sixteen and sixty) was extremely high—160.8 men to every 100 women. Consequently spinsters were few and they were generally propertyless dependents in the home of a male relative. Widows commonly remarried before their husbands had been buried a year—unless they were remarkably unattractive, elderly, or poor. Those in the last category, who could not support themselves on one-third of their deceased husband's estate, would be subject to the poor laws unless a male relative could be found to take them in. The poor law prescribed compulsory labor for the poor so that impoverished widows might be bound out to serve as domestics. In Wareham, Massachusetts (admittedly an exceptional case) there was an annual auction of indigent widows.

Americans under the age of twenty-one, a clear majority of the population in 1776, were legal infants, and the right to liberty of such persons was far from self-evident to the founding fathers, although they were aware that it seemed to follow, at least for older children, from the Lockean premises. It would be a mistake to confuse the class of legal minors in Revolutionary America with modern adolescents. Blackstone declared a boy of twelve fit to take an oath of allegience and a girl of seven ready to be given in marriage. The age of discretion for most purposes fell between seven and fourteen and all children above this age group were subject to capital punishment for felonies and bore most of the responsibilities if not the privileges of adults. Children entered the labor force well before they entered their teens, and they developed a degree of maturity and experience in the world that would be considered unhealthily precocious today. The large number of men in their early twenties who served competently as field officers in the Revolutionary armies and sat in the Continental Congresses could only have appeared in a society that considered teenage boys adults even though it deprived them of full legal rights. Male children of the age of sixteen were taxable and liable for militia duty. And since the population of colonial America was generally young, sixteen being the median age, unfree males between sixteen and twenty-one comprised one quarter of the total taxable male population. In an age when the mortality rates among infants and children were high and when a youth of sixteen had less than an even chance of surviving to the age of thirty, the loss of even a few years of liberty was a significant grievance.

Furthermore, theories of child nurture in colonial days were distinctly grim, based on the still formidable patriarchical traditions that had prescribed death for a "rebellious and incorrigible son." Obedience to parents was a duty imposed by divine as well as human law to be enforced by corporal punishment if necessary. Minors were expected to work for their parents as soon as they could walk, but they had no personal property rights before they came of legal age. Authority over children above ten or fourteen was frequently transferred from the natural parents to a master. The institution of apprenticeship was still viable at the time of the Revolution and was the usual path for a young man who did not intend to become a farmer but wished to learn a trade. Girls might also become apprenticed. Apprenticeship articles were drawn to standards set by colonial legislatures and generally required the consent of the child as well as of his parents. But children of poor or otherwise incompetent parents might be sold against their will to masters who promised, sometimes de-

ceitfully, to provide for them adequately and teach them a trade before they came of age.

Once apprenticed, a child's labor belonged to the master as fully as did that of any servant. Even visits to his own parents could be forbidden and the free-time conduct of apprentices was subject to the same sort of restrictions that applied to adult servants or slaves. Disobedience to a master as to a father could be punished with the whip. If a child came to detest the trade his father apprenticed him to, or if the master failed to make him proficient in the craft, his entire future would be warped, for once of age and free it would be too late to begin again to acquire the skills needed to make a living.

These four groups—Negroes, servants, women, and minors—together comprised approximately 80 percent of the two and a half million Americans in the year 1776. The legal doctrine applied to these classes excluded them from the category of persons who should enjoy the "inalienable rights" of which the Declaration speaks. But perhaps the most significant mark of their unfreedom was their usual lack of a right to vote, for the privilege of consenting to the laws was the essential right of a free man in Lockean theory. Indeed, the very word "enfranchise" was defined in the eighteenth century as the equivalent of the word "emancipate"; it meant "to make free."

Interestingly enough, the prohibition on the suffrage does not appear to have been absolute either in law or in fact for any of the unfree groups. Colonial suffrage legislation tended to be vague. Only Virginia, South Carolina, and Georgia specifically confined the franchise to white voters and there are recorded cases of Negroes, mulattoes, and Indians actually casting ballots. When in 1778 a provision excluding blacks from the suffrage was inserted in the proposed Massachusetts constitution, a citizen observed in the *Independent Chronicle* that "A black, tawny or reddish skin is not so unfavorable in hue to the genuine son of liberty, as a tory complection." Rare instances of bond servants casting votes are known and enough servants presumed to exercise the franchise in Albany, New York to necessitate their specific exclusion from participation in city elections in 1773.

Only Pennsylvania, Delaware, South Carolina, and Georgia specifically disfranchised females who otherwise qualified as property holders. When Hannah Lee Corbin protested to her brother Richard Henry Lee in 1778 that Virginia women ought not to be taxed if they had not the right to vote, he replied that "women were already possessed of that right," and, apparently, some women did vote for a time in Virginia as well as in New England and the middle colonies. But these cases were rare and it is significant that Mrs. Corbin did not know she had the franchise until her brother so informed her.

Only six states explicitly stated that voters must be twenty-one years of age (Pennsylvania, South Carolina, Virginia, Connecticut, New York, and North Carolina), and there are recorded cases of young men under legal age occasionally registering their votes.

In all likelihood, however, the liberality of colonial suffrage legislation was due to careless draftsmanship rather than to any desire to permit members of the unfree classes to vote. The intention was to limit the franchise to free, adult, white males and others who voted slipped through by accident as a result of laxity among election inspectors. Indeed, we know of such cases chiefly because they served as grounds for complaint in disputed elections.

A fifth group of colonial Americans, adult white males with little or no property, was deprived of the vote in colonial elections and so fell short of full liberty in the Lockean sense. But they were privileged above the other unfree groups since they were legally entitled to acquire property and were protected from physical abuse except such as was administered by public authority after trial as punishment for offenses against the state. Some of these disfranchised males were idiots, invalids, or residents of workhouses. Others were simply too poor to qualify under the arbitrary property requirements of the various electoral laws. Statistically they are the least significant of the unfree, although they have had more than their share of attention from critics of consensus history. They made up between 5 and 10 percent of the total population. If they are added to the 80 percent of the population in the other unfree categories, which were limited not merely in their political rights but in their rights to personal liberty and property as well, then only 10 to 15 percent of the American population remain to qualify as "freemen" in the fullest sense.

It is curious that this startling statistic has somehow escaped comment by historians. While the enslavement of Negroes and disfranchisement of some adult white males may be noted in passing as undemocratic elements in pre-Revolutionary America, the disfranchisement and worse of the other unfree classes is accepted without remark even in our enlightened age. Thus, Elisha P. Douglass defines democracy in his *Rebels and Democrats* as "a political system in which all adult males enjoyed equal political rights." Robert Brown writes in *Middle-Class Democracy and the Revolution in Massachusetts,* "The only valid approach . . . is to find out how many adult men could vote out of the total adult male population," and he concludes that "If anything with the appearance of a man could vote there was little problem of a restricted electorate." And finally, the author of this paper casually observed in *The Eleventh Pillar,* "The important ratio is that of qualified voters to adult white males."

Today almost 65 percent of the total population is enfranchised and in law, at least, virtually all of the people are secured in property rights and protected from physical abuse by private parties. Yet even our age finds it self-evident that women and young people should have been excluded from colonial political life. Since this is the case, we should not find it difficult to understand how the men of two centuries ago could accept the contradiction between their Lockean principles and their discriminatory practice without too much discomfort.

It would be both uncharitable and simplistic to dismiss the founding fathers as hypocrites because they tolerated this inconsistency. Some conflict between ideal principles and social practice is inevitable if the ideals are at all noble and the society composed of human beings rather than angels. Nor is such contradiction undesirable. Quite the opposite, since it induces men, who will always fall short of perfection in their day to day experience, to consider the possibility of alternative social arrangements superior to their own. Thus John Adams was vastly amused when his Abigail presumed to apply the Revolutionary slogans to the condition of married ladies. But after puzzling over her remarks for a month he realized that, indeed, he could discover no moral foundation for government that would justify the exclusion of any class of people from full participation. Of course it was "impossible," he wrote to James Sullivan, that the principle of consent should ever be carried so far. But the logic was undeniable and if it were followed to its conclusion "women will demand a vote; lads from twelve to twenty-one will think their rights not enough attended to: and every man who has not a farthing, will demand an equal voice with any other, in all acts of state." Adams seems to have predicted the long range impact of the Revolutionary doctrine accurately enough.

Again, Patrick Henry, facing up to the contrast between his words and his practice of keeping slaves, wrote, "I will not, I cannot justify it. However culpable my conduct, I will so far pay my devoir to virtue, as to own the excellence and rectitude of her precepts, and lament my want of conformity to them."

In the final analysis, however, the contradiction was tolerable to Americans because they compared the extent of liberty in their society not with the Lockean ideal but with the extent of liberty in other contemporary or historically known societies. From this perspective there was no doubt that the Americans of 1776 were remarkably free. Even the slaves, servants, women, and children of America enjoyed positions superior to those held by similar classes in other lands and other times. And surely a land in which more than 10 percent of the population owned property and had a voice in the government was a wonder in an age when the civilized world was ruled by hereditary monarchs and property ownership was a prerogative of aristocrats. Even in England, where the political liberty of the early eighteenth century had made her people the envy of Europe, no more than 25 percent of "the active male population" had voted in even the freest parts of the kingdom—and after the first third of the century even this electorate had dwindled. Yet, to quote J. H. Plumb, "this was England's vast singularity, a unique situation amongst the major powers of the world."

Surely the gap that separated American society from the Lockean ideal was no more impressive than that which separated colonial American society from the societies of Europe. If freedom had a home anywhere in the world in the year 1776 it was in the new United States of America. But if "democracy" implies government by consent of the governed or at least by consent of a majority of those governed and not merely of an adult white male elite, then those historians from Bancroft to Brown who have described American society of the mid-eighteenth century as "democratic" are simply wrong. The opinion of Carl Becker and many others that colonial governments "did in a rough and ready way, conform to the kind of government for which Locke furnished a reasoned foundation" is vastly overstated. And the attempts of the New Left history to view the American Revolution "from the bottom up" will be superficial so long as "the bottom" is conceived in a way that still excludes the majority of the population.

The People, Crowds, and Violence

GORDON S. WOOD (b. 1933) is best-known among historians for *The Creation of the American Republic, 1776–1787*, which focuses on the emergence and the impact of republican ideology on Revolutionary America. Before that volume appeared in 1969, Wood looked at other ways in which political ideology seemed to influence group behavior, most notably in the case of the Revolutionary crowds. Wood discusses the parallels between European and American crowds and suggests that the traditions of one often were also those of the other. American crowds during the Revolution seemed to be working to protect community interests against presumed malefactors of liberty. In light of that explanation, Wood calls for a new investigation of early American mob violence with the focus on the structure of a society that would encourage rather than suppress violent demonstrations.

# The Crowd in the American Revolution

There used to be a time when we thought that mob violence in the pre-industrial age of the eighteenth century was strictly a European phenomenon. In recent years, however, we have been made increasingly aware of how important and prevalent mob activity was in early American history. From the time of the first settlements on through the eighteenth century, social eruptions and popular disturbances were a recurrent event in the American colonies. Mob rioting at one time or another paralyzed all the major cities; and in the countryside violent uprisings of aggrieved farmers periodically destroyed property, closed courts, and brought government to a halt. With such a history of popular disturbances in the colonies it was not surprising then that mob action would become, as the Tories pointed out, "a necessary ingredient" in fomenting the American Revolution. "Mass violence," Arthur M. Schlesinger reminded us in 1955, "played a dominant role at every significant turning point of the events leading up to the War for Independence.

From Gordon S. Wood, "A Note on Mobs in the American Revolution," *William and Mary Quarterly*, 3rd Sers., XXIII (1966), pp. 635–642. Reprinted by permission of the author. Footnotes omitted.

Mobs terrified the stamp agents into resigning and forced a repeal of the tax. Mobs obstructed the execution of the Townshend Revenue Act and backed up the boycotts of British trade. Mobs triggered the Boston Massacre and later the famous Tea Party." And even after the Revolution had begun "civilian mobs behind the lines systematically intimidated Tory opponents, paralyzing their efforts or driving them into exile." In short, the American colonies were no more free of urban and rural riots and disturbances than eighteenth-century England and France.

Yet while recognizing that eighteenth-century crowd disturbances were as prevalent in the colonies as in Europe, almost all historical accounts of American mob activity have suggested that the colonial mobs were fundamentally different from their European counterparts. True, the American Revolution produced mob violence, but these crowd disturbances, most historians imply, were by no means comparable to the popular uprisings during the French Revolution, or even to the various English mob demonstrations during the same period. The American mobs seem to have behaved in a particularly unusual fashion, and in contrast to the violent uprisings of eighteenth-century Europe they appear to be hardly mobs at all.

Apparently in order to distinguish the American from the European crowds of the eighteenth century, historians have usually emphasized the middle-class character of the colonial mobs. "It is evident," Carl Bridenbaugh has written, "that in American cities those who constituted the mob, so called, were far from being a mere 'rabble'

seeking bread and an opportunity to release pent-up boorish boisterousness by despoiling the Egyptians." Indeed, "the contrast with the still medieval English mob is striking in that the colonial variety had in them always a majority of middle-class citizens and the approval of many more." Bridenbaugh has concluded, however, as has Bernard Bailyn in a more recent note on American mobs, that the American crowds possessed many real "deeply rooted, popular grievances" which found expression in general political issues and principles, a conclusion which by itself has important and unsettling implications for our traditional assumption about the character of American mob behavior. In his comprehensive account of the mob violence surrounding the Stamp Act and its marked effectiveness in pressuring the stamp distributors into resigning, Edmund S. Morgan has given us a somewhat different view, denying that the mobs were the "spontaneous outbursts of the rabble," and picturing them more as passive bodies of men manipulated by their socially superior leaders; indeed "the episodes of violence which defeated the Stamp Act in America were planned and prepared by men who were recognized at the time as belonging to the better and wiser part." So extraordinary in fact were the mobs' discipline and discrimination in the destruction of property that Morgan was led into a noticeably sympathetic description ("the previous evening's entertainment") of the mob violence. The American Revolutionary mob, Lloyd Rudolph has concluded in a pointed comparison of eighteenth-century European and colonial mobs, demonstrated particular restraint "in confining its activities to specific and limited objectives. . . . In America, the mob stopped when it had attained what it set out to do." The rioters destroyed only property, and particularly selected property, and took no, or few, lives during the Revolution. "Heads did not roll in the American Revolution," wrote Bailyn; "mobs did not turn to butchery." "A singular self-restraint characterized the frenzies," declared Schlesinger, "for the participants invariably stopped short of death." In short, as Rudolph has summarized, the American mob, like the Revolution of which it was a part, was remarkably moderate and disciplined. It was "never swept up into an irrational destruction of lives and property." Thus America was "spared from the mob in the European sense of the word." Indeed, it seems to be the assumed conclusion of all historians of eighteenth-century American crowd disturbances that it was only "in Europe that the real mob existed."

But what actually is a "real mob," a mob "in the European sense of the word"? It would seem that our image of the eighteenth-century European mob has been very impressionistic and hasty, but understandably so, since only in recent years have scholars begun to study the preindustrial European crowds with care and sympathy, investigating them not as static abstractions but as concrete historical and social phenomena, seeing them not as the authorities saw them, but as they were to the participants. One of the boldest and most prolific of these scholars is George Rudé, who has recently sought to bring together his several studies of the European crowd into a more general discussion,

entitled *The Crowd in History: A Study of Popular Disturbances in France and England, 1730–1848.* Speculative as Rudé's conclusions about the European crowd may be, they still have interest and significance for all historians; but they have a special relevance for students of the American Revolution, for in effect they call into question the assumptions about the unique quality of the American mobs in the eighteenth century.

Far from discovering the irrational, fickle, and destructive abstractions described by Gustave Le Bon, the father of modern crowd psychology, and others, Rudé found the eighteenth-century English and French crowds to be usually rational with a "remarkable single-mindedness and discriminating purposefulness." "In fact," he writes, "the study of the pre-industrial crowd suggests that it rioted for precise objects and rarely engaged in indiscriminate attacks on either properties or persons." The Gordon Riots of 1780, for example, were "directed against carefully selected targets," and "considerable care was taken to avoid damage to neighboring property." Moreover, those who assume that the mobs "have no worthwhile aspirations of their own and, being naturally venal, can be prodded into activity only by the promise of a reward by outside agents or 'conspirators' " are greatly mistaken. The crowd's motives were diverse and complicated, ranging from the seeking of "elementary social justice at the expense of the rich, *les grands,* and those in authority" to the devotion to political principles and generalized beliefs about man's place in society. Such complex goals reflected the varied composition of the crowds. For the crowds of eighteenth-century England and France, even the French Revolutionary mobs, were not composed of the riffraff of society, but rather represented a fair cross section of the working class together with some petty employees and craftsmen occasionally interspersed with men of "the better sort." Nor were the preindustrial crowds bloodthirsty. According to Rudé the usually selective destruction of property was a constant characteristic, "but not the destruction of human lives." There were notably few fatalities among the rioters' victims. In the week-long Gordon Riots not a single person was killed by the mobs. And, in fact, "the French Revolution in Paris, for all the destructive violence that attended it, was not particularly marked by murderous violence on the part of crowds." Most of those who died during the European demonstrations were rioters killed by the magistracy or the army. "It was authority rather than the crowd," Rudé concludes, "that was conspicuous for its violence to life and limb."

What is particularly striking about Professor Rudé's analysis of the eighteenth-century European crowd is its resemblance to the description of the American Revolutionary mobs that we have been used to. When viewed in light of Rudé's study, eighteenth-century American crowd behavior loses much of its distinctiveness. It now becomes more difficult to emphasize the peculiar rationality and discrimination of American mobs in their treatment of property. It is also hard to see how they were composed of more respectable, middle-class elements than their European counterparts. And it appears especially distorting to stress

the unusual moderation and respect for lives displayed by American crowds. It seems misleading, in short, to conclude that during the American Revolutionary crisis "no mob action approached the mayhem and destruction of French and English mobs of roughly the same period."

Nevertheless the historical and social situation and the consequences of mob violence in America were very different from those in Europe, and it would be distorting the very basis of Rudé's studies to ignore these differences. Eighteenth-century American society had neither the complexity nor the number of grievances possessed by eighteenth-century French society. In the colonies there were no bread riots, no uprisings of the destitute. Yet, as Rudé has pointed out, it was not really poverty that precipitated rioting in Europe. Many of the disturbances occurred in times of greatest prosperity; even the food riots were not the product of long-suffering deprivation but of temporary price rises and shortages. Rudé's study suggests that the preindustrial demonstrations represented not the anarchic uprisings of the poor and hopeless but rather a form of political protest made both necessary and possible by the increasing democratization of a society lacking the proper institutions for either the successful expression or the swift repression of that protest. It is perhaps in this context that the American mobs can most instructively be viewed and compared with the European crowds. What particularly seems to set mob violence in the colonies apart from the popular disturbances in England and France is not so much the character of the mob, the purposeful and limited nature of its goals, its consideration for human life, or even the felt intensity of its grievances; rather it is the almost total absence of resistance by the constituted authorities, with all that this absence may signify in explaining the nature of the society and the consequences of the outbursts. If the institutions of law and order were weak in eighteenth-century England and France, in America they were unusually ineffectual. Scholars have emphasized time and again the helplessness of the imperial government when confronted by a colonial mob reinforced by widespread sympathy in the community. It was apparently more the restraint and timidity of the British authorities, and less the moderation of the American crowds, that prevented a serious loss of lives during the American rioting. The nearly complete breakdown of the royal government's ability to command support in the society in the years before independence worked to retard an aggravation of colonial grievances and a rapid escalation of killing and violence, but it did not make the American mob any less a mob.

Moreover, the weakness of the legally constituted authority in America did not end with the Declaration of Independence and the formation of new popular governments. The Whig belief in the people's "right of resistance" (which had often hampered magistrates in England dealing with mobs) became a justification for continued disorder in the years after 1776. Serious rioting recurred in many of the major cities and formed the background for the incorporation movements in Boston, New Haven, Philadelphia, and Charleston in 1780's. Extralegal groups and conventions repeatedly sprang up to take public action into their own hands, to intimidate voters, to regulate prices, or to close the courts. To some in the 1780's it seemed as though mobs were taking over the functions of government. This was not simply a chimerical fear, for the legislatures in the 1780's appeared to be extraordinarily susceptible to mass demonstrations and mob violence. The state governments were continually forced to submit to various kinds of popular pressures, often expressed outside the regular legal channels. In this atmosphere Shays's Rebellion represented something of an anomaly, largely because the farmers of western Massachusetts, unlike other groups in the 1780's, found no release for their pent-up grievances in legislative action but instead were forcefully resisted by the authorities. Connecticut had no violence like that of Massachusetts, said Noah Webster, "because the Legislature wear the complexion of the people." Only "the temporising of the legislatures in refusing legal protection to the prosecution of the just rights of creditors," remarked David Ramsay, freed the Southern states from similar disturbances. Within a few months, however, observers noted that the Shaysites were trying their strength in another way, "that is," said James Madison, "by endeavoring to give the elections such a turn as may promote their views under the auspices of Constitutional forms." With "a total change" of men in the legislature, wrote Webster, "there will be, therefore, no further insurrection, because the Legislature will represent the sentiments of the people." Some Americans in the 1780's could thus come to believe that "sedition itself will sometimes make law." Hence, it might be argued that it was the very weakness of the constituted authorities, their very susceptibility to popular intimidation of various kinds, or, in other words, the very democratic character of legislative politics in the 1780's, rather than any particular self-restraint or temperance in the people, that prevented the eruption of more serious violence during the Confederation period. If this is the case then our current conception of the period and our understanding of the Federalist movement may have to be reexamined.

What Professor Rudé's analysis of eighteenth-century European crowd requires at the very least, it seems, is a new look at American mob violence during the Revolution focusing on the structure of the society which prompts popular demonstrations and on the nature of the institutions which are compelled to deal with them. If the conservatism of the American mobs is not as peculiar as we once assumed, if the crowds were not simply the passive instruments of outside agents, we must learn more about their composition, their goals, and the sources of their discontents. Particularly we need to know more about the circumstances and consequences of repression or the absence of it. In short, in light of Rudé's findings the obvious differences between mob action in America and in Europe that do exist demand a broader and yet more precise explanation than we have had. It is not enough now to say that the nature of the American mob in and by itself was distinctive.

Moreover, if the mob is pictured as a kind of microcosm of the Revolution, Rudé's studies may even have wider implications. Perhaps the American Revolution was as moderate as it seems, so lacking in the violence and ferocity of the French Revolution, not because it was inherently conservative and unrevolutionary, led by law-abiding men with limited objectives, but rather because it was so unrestrained, so lacking in strong resistance from counterrevolutionary and authoritarian elements, and consequently so successfully revolutionary. Unchecked by any serious internal opposition, unrestrained by any solid institutional bulwarks, the American Revolutionaries may have ultimately carried themselves further in the transformation of their society, although without the bloodshed or the terror, then even the French Revolutionaries were eventually able to do. For if the American mob was no less a mob because of the absence of effective resistance, was the Revolution any less a revolution?

JESSE LEMISCH (b. 1936) is one of a group of "New Left" historians who have called for fundamental revisions in the way American history is written. Rather than presuming that the words of the elite accurately reflected everyone else's needs and thoughts, Lemisch has suggested that the past be viewed "from the bottom up," that is, from the perspective of the "historically silent" masses who did not leave written records behind. In proving that such research was possible, Lemisch concentrated on the "Jack Tars," the common seamen of Revolutionary America. He concluded that violence was the only means by which this unenfranchised group could express its anger and protest its grievances. Ironically, the common seamen gained nothing from the Revolutionary experience. Why did they work with other proponents of large-scale resistance, then? Were they seeking an internal social revolution or did they want something else, such as full participatory inclusion in the new system?

# Jack Tar in the Streets

Here comes Jack Tar, his bowed legs bracing him as if the very Broadway beneath his feet might begin to pitch and roll. In his dress he is, in the words of a superior, "very nasty and negligent," his black stockings ragged, his long, baggy trousers tarred to make them waterproof. Bred in "that very shambles of language," the merchant marine, he is foul-mouthed, his talk alien and suspect. He is Jolly Jack, a bull in a china shop, always, in his words, "for a Short Life and a Merry one," and, in the concurring words of his superiors, "concerned only for the present . . . incapable of thinking of, or inattentive to, future welfare," "like froward Children not knowing how to judge for themselves."

Clothes don't make the man, nor does language; surely we can do better than these sterotypes. Few have tried. Maritime history, as it has been written, has had as little to do with the common seaman as business history has to do with the laborer. In that *mischianza* of mystique and elitism, "seaman" has meant Sir Francis Drake,

From Jesse Lemisch, "Jack Tar in the Streets: Merchant Seamen in the Politics of Revolutionary America," *William and Mary Quarterly*, 3rd Sers., XXV (1968), pp. 371–407. Copyright© 1968 by Jesse Lemisch. Reprinted by permission of the author. Footnotes omitted.

not Jack Tar; the focus has been on trade, exploration, the great navigators, but rarely on the men who sailed the ships. Thus we know very little about Jack. Samuel Eliot Morison is one of the few who have tried to portray the common seaman. In an influential anecdote in *The Maritime History of Massachusetts* Morison has described a "frequent occurrence" in early New England. A farmer's boy, called by the smell or the sight of the sea, suddenly runs off; three years later he returns as a man, marries the hired girl, and lives "happily ever after." This experience, Morison tells us, was "typical of the Massachusetts merchant marine," where the "old salt" was almost non-existent and where there never was "a native deep-sea proletariat." The ships were sailed by wave after wave of "adventure-seeking boys," drawn by high wages and *wanderlust.* If they recovered, they took their earnings, married, and bought a farm; if not, these "young, ambitious seamen culled from the more active element of a pushing race" stayed on and rose to become masters in a merchant marine distinguished from its class-ridden European counterparts by easy mobility.

There is much to support Morison's *tableau.* Even if the mystique of the sea has been no more than mystique, still it has existed and exerted a powerful force. Washington, Franklin, and thousands of others did suffer attacks of "sea fever." Seamen were, as Morison says, young men, averaging in one sample slightly over twenty-four, with many like John Paul Jones who went to sea at thirteen and even some who went at eight. Many of them "hove in hard at the Hause-hole" and became masters of their own vessels;

later, while their sons and grandsons added to their wealth, they retired, perhaps to their farms, and wrote proud histories of their successes. Some, like Nicholas Biddle, found the navy a better outlet for their ambitions than the merchant service. Others, following Morison's pattern, quit the sea early and turned to farming. For many there was mobility between generations and between trades. Seamen and landsmen might be distinct classes in Europe, but in America, men such as Albert Gallatin who knew both the Old World and the New found no "material distinction." So Jack Tar seems to have been simply the landsman gone to sea, indistinguishable from his fellows ashore, and, together with them, on his way to prosperity.

If the seaman was a clean young farm-boy on the make—and likely to succeed—why was Josiah Franklin so apprehensive lest young Benjamin "break loose and go to sea"? Why did Josiah fight his son's "strong inclination to go to sea" by frantically trying to make of him a joiner, a bricklayer, a turner, a brazier, a tallow-chandler, a cutler, a printer—anything, so long as it would keep him on land? Why did Washington's uncle suggest that young George would better become a planter or even an apprentice to a tinker, while explicitly urging that he not become a seaman?

"All masters of vessels are warned not to harbor, conceal, or employ him, as they will answer for it, as the law directs." To a fleeing apprentice, dissatisfied with the "bondage" of work ashore, to a runaway slave, the sea might appear the only real shelter. Men with no experience at sea tried to pass for seamen and before long discovered that they had indeed become seamen. Others *were* seamen, apprenticed in one vessel and fled to another. Still others, deserted soldiers, bail-jumpers, thieves, and murderers, had gotten into trouble with the law. And others went to sea entirely unwillingly, originally impressed—perhaps from jail—into the navy, or tricked into the merchant service by crimps. These were the floaters who drifted and slipped their moorings, the suicides, the men whose wives—if they had wives—ran off with other men; the beneficiaries in their wills—when they left wills—were innkeepers. Hitherto, argued a proponent of a United States navy in 1782, the merchant marine had been "the resource of necessity, accident or indulgence."

The merchant marine was a place full of forces beyond the seaman's control: death and disease, storms, and fluctuations in employment. Indeed, the lack of "old salts" in Morison's merchant marine might reflect a sombre irony: was the average seaman young because mobility rapidly brought him to another trade or because seamen died young? A man in jail, said Dr. Johnson, was at least safe from drowning, and he had more room, better food, and better company. The Quaker John Woolman was one of the few sensitive enough to see that if the "poor bewildered sailors" drank and cursed, the fault lay not so much in themselves as in the harsh environment and the greed of employers. Nor was the road up through the hawse-hole so easy as Morison asserts. That the few succeeded tells us nothing of the many; only the successful left autobiographies. Perhaps the sons of merchants and ship-masters made it, along with the captain's brother-in-law and those who attended schools of navigation, but what of the "poor lads bound apprentice" who troubled Woolman, those whose wages went to their masters? What of the seamen in Morison's own Boston who died too poor to pay taxes and who were a part of what James Henretta has called "the bottom" of Boston society? What of those who went bankrupt with such frequency in Rhode Island? Why, at the other end of the colonies, did Washington's uncle warn that it would be "very difficult" to become master of a Virginia vessel and not worth trying?

The presence of such men, fugitives and floaters, powerless in a tough environment, makes *wanderlust* appear an ironic parody of the motives which made at least some men go to sea. Catch the seaman when he is not pandering to your romanticism, said former seaman Frederick Law Olmsted a century later, and he will tell you that he hates the sight of blue water, he hates his ship, his officers, and his messmates—and he despises himself. Melville's Ishmael went to sea when he felt grim, hostile, and suicidal: "It is a way I have of driving off the spleen." No matter what we make of Ishmael, we cannot possibly make him into one of Morison's "adventure-seeking boys." Others, perhaps, but not Ishmael. The feelings of eighteenth-century Americans toward seafaring and seamen, and what evidence we have of the reasons men had for going to sea indicate that there were many like Ishmael in the colonial period, too, who left the land in flight and fear, outcasts, men with little hope of success ashore. These were the dissenters from the American mood. Their goals differed from their fellows ashore; these were the rebels, the men who stayed on to become old salts.

Admiralty law treated seamen in a special way, as "wards." Carl Ubbelohde says that seamen favored the colonial Vice Admiralty Courts as "particular tribunals in case of trouble," and Charles M. Andrews and Richard B. Morris agreed that these courts were "guardians of the rights of the seamen." The benefits of being classified as a "ward" are dubious, but, regardless of the quality of treatment which admiralty law accorded to seamen, it certainly does not follow that, all in all, the colonial seaman was well treated by the law. Indeed, if we broaden our scope to include colonial law generally, we find an extraordinarily harsh collection of laws, all justifying Olmsted's later claim that American seamen "are more wretched, and are governed more by threats of force than any other civilized laborers of the world." There are laws providing for the whipping of disobedient seamen and in one case for their punishment as "seditious"; laws prohibiting seamen in port from leaving their vessels after sundown and from travelling on land without certificates of discharge from their last job; laws empowering "every free white person" to catch runaway seamen. We find other laws, less harsh, some seeming to protect the seaman: laws against extending credit to seamen and against arresting them for debt, and against entertaining them in taverns for more than one hour per day; laws against selling them liquor and prohibiting them from playing with cards or dice; laws waiving imprisonment for seamen convicted

of cursing; laws requiring masters to give discharge certificates to their seamen and laws prohibiting hiring without such certificates. Finally, there are laws which clearly do help the seaman: laws requiring masters to provide "good and sufficient diet and accommodation" and providing for redress if the master refused; laws providing punishment for masters who "immoderately beat, wound, or maim" their seamen; laws providing that seamen's contracts be written.

These harsh or at best paternalistic laws add up to a structure whose purpose is to assure a ready supply of cheap, docile labor. Obedience, both at sea and ashore, is the keystone. Charles Beard at his most rigidly mechanistic would doubtless have found the Constitution merely mild stuff alongside this blatantly one-sided class legislation. Today's historians of the classless society would do well to examine the preambles of these laws, written in a more candid age, by legislatures for which, even by Robert Brown's evidence, most seamen could not vote. Again and again these laws aim to inhibit acts of seamen which may do "prejudice to masters and owners of vessells" or constitute a "manifest detriment of . . . trade." The seamen's interests are sacrificed to the merchants', and even the laws which seem friendly to the seaman benefit the master. Laws against giving credit, arresting, and suing aim to keep the seaman available rather than involved in a lawsuit or imprisoned; the certificates and written contracts seek to prevent desertion and to protect the master against what would today be called a "strike"; the laws protecting seamen against immoderate punishment and requiring adequate food and accommodation are implicitly weak in that they require that dependents make open complaint against their superiors. Sometimes this limitation is made explicit, as in a South Carolina law of 1751 whose stated purpose is "TO DISCOURAGE FRIVOLOUS AND VEXATIOUS ACTIONS AT LAW BEING BROUGHT BY SEAMEN AGAINST MASTERS AND COMMANDERS."

Thus if we think of Jack Tar as jolly, childlike, irresponsible, and in many ways surprisingly like the Negro stereotype, it is because he was treated so much like a child, a servant, and a slave. What the employer saw as the necessities of an authoritarian profession were written into law and culture: the society that wanted Jack dependent made him that way and then concluded that that was the way he really was.

## II

Constantly plagued by short complements, the Royal Navy attempted to solve its manning problems in America, as in England, by impressment. Neil Stout has recently attributed these shortages to "death, illness, crime, and desertion" which were in turn caused largely by rum and by the deliberate enticements of American merchants. Rum and inveiglement certainly took a high toll, but to focus on these two causes of shortages is unfairly to shift the blame for impressment onto its victims. The navy itself caused shortages. Impressment, said Thomas Hutchinson, caused desertion, rather than the other way around. Jack Tar had good reasons for avoiding the navy. It would, a young Virginian was warned, "cut him and staple him and use him like a Negro, or rather, like a dog"; James Otis grieved at the loss of the "flower" of Massachusetts's youth "by ten thousands" to a service which treated them little better than "hewers of wood and drawers of water." Discipline was harsh and sometimes irrational, and punishments were cruel. Water poured into sailors' beds, they went mad, and died of fevers and

scurvy. Sickness, Benjamin Franklin noted, was more common in the navy than in the merchant service and more frequently fatal. In a fruitless attempt to prevent desertion, wages were withheld and men shunted about from ship to ship without being paid. But the accumulation of even three or four years' back wages could not keep a man from running. And why should it have? Privateering paid better in wartime, and wages were higher in the merchant service; even laborers ashore were better paid. Thus Stout's claim that the navy was "forced" to press is only as accurate as the claim that the South was forced to enslave Negroes. Those whose sympathies lie with the thousands of victims of this barbaric practice—rather than with naval administrators—will see that the navy pressed because to be in the navy was in some sense to be a slave, and for this we must blame the slave owners rather than the slaves.

Impressment angered and frightened the seamen, but it pervaded and disrupted all society, giving other classes and groups cause to share a common grievance with the press-gang's more direct victims: just about everyone had a relative at sea. Whole cities were crippled. A night-time operation in New York in 1757 took in eight hundred men, the equivalent of more than one-quarter of the city's adult male population. Impressment and the attendant shortage of men may have been a critical factor in the stagnancy of "the once cherished now depressed, once flourishing now sinking Town of Boston." H.M.S. *Shirley's* log lists at least ninety-two men pressed off Boston in five months of 1745–1746; *Gramont* received seventy-three pressed men in New York in three days in 1758; *Arethusa* took thirty-one in two days off Virginia in 1771. Binges such as these left the communities where they occurred seriously harmed. Preachers' congregations took flight, and merchants complained loudly about the "many Thousands of Pounds of Damage." "Kiss my arse, you dog," shouted the captain as he made off with their men, leaving vessels with their fires still burning, unmanned, finally to be wrecked. They took legislators and slaves, fishermen and servants. Seamen took to the woods or fled town altogether, dreading the appearance of a man-of-war's boat— in the words of one—as a flock of sheep dreaded a wolf's appearance. If they offered to work at all, they demanded inflated wages and refused to sail to ports where there was danger of impressment. "New York and Boston," Benjamin Franklin commented during the French and Indian War, "have so often found the Inconvenience of . . . Station Ships that they are very indifferent about having them: The Pressing of Their Men and thereby disappointing Voyages, often hurting their

Trade more than the Enemy hurts it." Even a ferryboat operator complained as people shunned the city during a press; food and fuel grew short and their prices rose.

From the very beginning the history of impressment in America is a tale of venality, deceit, and vindictiveness. Captains kept deserters and dead men on ships' books, pocketing their provision allowances. In 1706 a captain pressed men and literally sold them to short-handed vessels; his midshipman learned the business so well that after his dismissal he became a veritable entrepreneur of impressment, setting up shop in a private sloop. Another commander waited until New York's governor was away to break a no-press agreement and when the governor returned he seriously considered firing on the Queen's ship. In Boston in 1702 the lieutenant-governor did *fire*, responding to merchants' complaints. "Fire and be damn'd," shouted the impressing captain as the shots whistled through his sails. The merchants had complained that the press was illegal under 1697 instructions which required captains and commanders to apply to colonial governors for permission to press. These instructions, a response to complaints of "irregular proceedings of the captains of some of our ships of war in the impressing of seamen," had clearly not put an end to irregularities. In 1708 a Parliament fearful of the disruptive effect of impressment on trade forbade the practice in America. In the sixty-seven years until the repeal in 1775 of this "Act for the Encouragement of the Trade of America" there was great disagreement as to its meaning and indeed as to its very existence. Did the Sixth of Anne, as the act was called, merely prohibit the navy from impressing and leave governors free to do so? At least one governor, feeling "pinioned" under the law, continued impressing while calling it "borrowing." Was the act simply a wartime measure, which expired with the return of peace in 1713? Regardless of the dispute, impressment continued, routine in its regularity, but often spectacular in its effects.

Boston was especially hard-hit by impressment in the 1740's, with frequent incidents throughout the decade and major explosions in 1745 and 1747. Again and again the town meeting and the House of Representatives protested, drumming away at the same themes: impressment was harmful to maritime commerce and to the economic life of the city in general and illegal if not properly authorized. In all this the seaman himself becomes all but invisible. The attitude towards him in the protests is at best neutral and often sharply antagonistic. In 1747 the House of Representatives condemned the violent response of hundreds of seamen to a large-scale press as "a tumultuous riotous assembling of armed Seamen, Servants, Negroes, and others . . . tending to the Destruction of all Government and Order." While acknowledging that the people had reason to protest, the House chose to level *its* protest against "the most audacious Insult" to the governor, Council, and House. And the town meeting, that stronghold of democracy, offered its support to those who took "orderly" steps while expressing its "Abhorence of such Illegal Criminal Proceedings" as those undertaken by seamen "and other persons of mean and Vile Condition."

Protests such as these reflect at the same time both unity and division in colonial society. All kinds of Americans —both merchants and seamen—opposed impressment, but the town meeting and the House spoke for the merchant, not the seaman. They opposed impressment not for its effect on the seaman but for its effect on commerce. Thus their protests express antagonism to British policy at the same time that they express class division. These two themes continue and develop in American opposition to impressment in the three decades between the Knowles Riots of 1747 and the Declaration of Independence.

During the French and Indian War the navy competed with privateers for seamen. Boston again protested against impressment, and then considered authorizing the governor to press, "provided said Men be impressed from inward-bound Vessels from Foreign Parts only, and that none of them be Inhabitants of this Province." In 1760 New York's mayor had a naval captain arrested on the complaint of two shipmasters who claimed that he had welched on a deal to exchange two men he had pressed for two others they were willing to furnish. With the return of peace in 1763 admirals and Americans alike had reason to suppose that there would be no more impressment. But the Admiralty's plan for a large new American fleet required otherwise, and impressment began again in the spring of 1764 in New York, where a seven-week hot press was brought to a partial stop by the arrest of one of the two offending captains. In the spring and summer a hunt for men between Maine and Virginia by four naval vessels brought violent responses, including the killing of a marine at New York; another fort, at Newport, fired on another naval vessel.

Along with the divisions there was a certain amount of unity. Seamen who fled after violently resisting impressment could not be found—probably because others sheltered them—and juries would not indict them. Captains were prevented from impressing by the threat of prosecution. And in 1769 lawyer John Adams used the threat of displaying the statute book containing the Sixth of Anne to frighten a special court of Admiralty into declaring the killing of an impressing lieutenant justifiable homicide in necessary self-defense.

There were two kinds of impressment incidents: those in which there was immediate self-defense against impressment, usually at sea, and those in which crowds ashore, consisting in large part of seamen, demonstrated generalized opposition to impressment. This is what the first kind of incident sounded like: a volley of musketry and the air full of langrage, grapeshot, round shot, hammered shot, double-headed shot, even rocks. "Come into the boat and be damned, you Sorry Son of a Whore or else Ile breake your head, and hold your tongue." Small arms, swords and cutlasses, blunderbusses, clubs and pistons, axes, harpoons, fishgigs, twelve-pounders, six-pounders, half-pounders. "You are a parsill of Raskills." Fired five shots to bring to a snow from North Carolina, pressed four. "You have no right to impress me . . . If you step over that line . . . by the eternal God of Heaven, you are a dead man." "Aye, my lad, I have seen many a brave fellow before

now."

Here is hostility and bloodshed, a tradition of antagonism. From the beginning, impressment's most direct victims—the seamen—were its most active opponents. Bernard Bailyn's contention that "not a single murder resulted from the activities of the Revolutionary mobs in America" does not hold up if extended to cover resistance to impressment; there were murders on both sides. Perhaps the great bulk of incidents of this sort must remain forever invisible to the historian, for they often took place out of sight of friendly observers, and the only witness, the navy, kept records which are demonstrably biased and faulty, omitting the taking of thousands of men. But even the visible records provide a great deal of information. This much we know without doubt: seamen did not go peacefully. Their violence was purposeful, and sometimes they were articulate. "I know who you are," said one, as reported by John Adams and supported by Thomas Hutchinson. "You are the lieutenant of a man-of-war, come with a press-gang to deprive me of my liberty. You have no right to impress me. I have retreated from you as far as I can. I can go no farther. I and my companions are determined to stand upon our defence. Stand off." (It was difficult for Englishmen to fail to see impressment in such terms—even a sailor *doing* the pressing could feel shame over "fighting with honest sailors, to deprive them of their liberty.")

Ashore, seamen and others demonstrated their opposition to impressment with the only weapon which the unrepresentative politics of the day offered them—riot. In Boston several thousand people responded to a night-time impressment sweep of the harbor and docks with three days of rioting beginning in the early hours of November 17, 1747. Thomas Hutchinson reported that "the lower class were beyond measure enraged." Negroes, servants, and hundreds of seamen seized a naval lieutenant, assulted a sheriff and put his deputy in the stocks, surrounded the governor's house, and stormed the Town House where the General Court was sitting. The rioters demanded the seizure of the impressing officers, the release of the men they had pressed, and execution of a death sentence which had been levied against a member of an earlier press-gang who had been convicted to murder. When the governor fled to Castle William—some called it "abdication"—Commodore Knowles threatened to put down what he called "arrant rebellion" by bombarding the town. The governor, who, for his part, thought the rioting a secret plot of the upper class, was happily surprised when the town meeting expressed its "Abhorence" of the seamen's riot.

After the French and Indian War press riots increased in frequency. Armed mobs of whites and Negroes repeatedly manhandled captains, officers, and crews, threatened their lives, and held them hostage for the men they pressed. Mobs fired at pressing vessels and tried to board them; they threatened to burn one, and they regularly dragged ships' boats to the center of town for ceremonial bonfires. In Newport in June 1765, five hundred seamen, boys, and Negroes rioted after five weeks of impressment. "Sensible" Newporters opposed impressment but nonetheless condemned this "Rabble." In Norfolk in 1767 Captain Jeremiah Morgan retreated, sword in hand, before a mob of armed whites and Negroes. "Good God," he wrote to the governor, "was your Honour and I to prosecute all the Rioters that attacked us belonging to Norfolk there would not be twenty left unhang'd belonging to the Toun." According to Thomas Hutchinson, the *Liberty* Riot in Boston in 1768 may have been as much against impressment as against the seizure of Hancock's sloop: *Romney* had pressed before June 10, and on that day three officers were forced by an angry crowd "arm'd with Stones" to release a man newly pressed from the Boston packet. *Romney* pressed another man, and on June 14, after warding off "many wild and violent proposals," the town meeting petitioned the governor against both the seizure and impressment; the instructions to their representatives (written by John Adams) quoted the Sixth of Anne at length. On June 18 two councillors pleaded with the governor to procure the release of a man pressed by *Romney* "as the peace of the Town seems in a great measure to depend upon it."

There were other impressment riots at New York in July of 1764 and July of 1765; at Newport in July of 1764; at Casco Bay, Maine, in December 1764. Incidents continued during the decade following, and impressment flowered on the very eve of the Revolution. Early in 1775 the practice began to be used in a frankly vindictive and political way—because a town had inconvenienced an admiral, or because a town supported the Continental Congress. Impresses were ordered and took place from Maine to Virginia.

In September a bundle of press warrants arrived from the Admiralty, along with word of the repeal of the Sixth of Anne. What had been dubious was now legal. Up and down the coast, officers rejoiced and went to work.

Long before 1765 Americans had developed beliefs about impressment, and they had expressed those beliefs in words and deeds. Impressment was bad for trade and it was illegal. As such, it was, in the words of the Massachusetts House in 1720, "a great Breach on the Rights of His Majesties Subjects." In 1747 it was a violation of "the common Liberty of the Subject," and in 1754 "inconsistent with Civil Liberty, and the Natural Rights of Mankind." Some felt in 1757 that it was even "abhorrent to the English Constitution." In fact, the claim that impressment was unconstitutional was wrong. (Even *Magna Charta* was no protection. *Nullus liber homo capiatur* did not apply to seamen.) Instead impressment indicated to Benjamin Franklin "that the constitution is yet imperfect, since in so general a case it doth not secure liberty, but destroys it." "If impressing seamen is of right by common law in Britain," he also remarked, "slavery is then of right by common law there; there being no slavery worse than that sailors are subjected to."

For Franklin, impressment was a symptom of injustice built into the British Constitution. In *Common Sense* Tom Paine saw in impressment a reason for rejecting monarchy. In the Declaration of Independence Thomas Jefferson included impressment among the "Oppressions" of George III; later he likened the practice to the capture of Africans for slavery. Both "reduced [the victim] to . . . bondage by force, in flagrant violation of his own consent, and of his natural right in his own person."

Despite all this, and all that went before, we have thought little of impressment as an element in explaining the conduct of the common man in the American Revolution. Contemporaries knew better. John Adams felt that a tactical mistake by Thomas Hutchinson on the question of impressment in 1769 would have "accelerated the revolution. . . . It would have spread a wider flame than Otis's ever did, or could have done." Ten years later American seamen were being impressed by *American* officers. The United States Navy had no better solution for "public Necessities" than had the Royal Navy. Joseph Reed, President of Pennsylvania, complained to Congress of "Oppressions" and in so doing offered testimony to the role of *British* impressment in bringing on revolution. "We cannot help observing how similar this Conduct is to that of the British Officers during our Subjection to Great Britain and are persuaded it will have the same unhappy effects viz., an estrangement of the Affections of the People from the Authority under which they act which by an easy Progression will proceed to open Opposition to the immediate Actors and Bloodshed." Impressment had played a role in the estrangement of the American people from the British government. It had produced "Odium" against the navy, and even six-year-olds had not been too young to have learned to detest it. The anger of thousands of victims did not vanish. Almost four decades after the Declaration of Independence an orator could still arouse his audience by tapping a folk-memory of impressment by the same "haughty, cruel, and gasconading nation" which was once again trying to enslave free Americans.

III

The seamen's conduct in the 1760's and 1770's makes more sense in the light of previous and continued impressment. What may have seemed irrational violence can now be seen as purposeful and radical. The pattern of rioting as political expression, established as a response to impressment, was now adapted and broadened as a response to the Stamp Act. In New York General Gage described the "insurrection" of October 31, 1765, and following as "composed of great numbers of Sailors." The seamen, he said, were "the only People who may be properly Stiled Mob," and estimates indicate that between a fifth and a fourth of New York's rioters were seamen. The disturbances began among the seamen—especially former privateersmen—on October 31. On November 1 they had marched, led primarily by their former captains; later they rioted, led by no one but themselves. Why? Because they had been duped by merchants, or, if not by merchants, then certainly by lawyers. So British officials believed—aroused by these men who meant to use them, the seamen themselves had nothing more than plunder on their minds. In fact, at that point in New York's rioting when the leaders lost control, the seamen, who were then in the center of town, in an area rich for plunder, chose instead to march in an orderly and disciplined way clear across town to do violence to the home and possessions of an English major whose provocative conduct had made him the obvious political enemy. Thus the "rioting" was actually very discriminating.

Seamen and non-seamen alike joined to oppose the Stamp Act for many reasons, but the seamen had two special grievances: impressment and the effect of England's new attitude toward colonial trade. To those discharged by the navy at the end of the war and others thrown out of work by the death of privateering were added perhaps twenty thousand more seamen and fishermen who were thought to be the direct victims of the post-1763 trade regulations. This problem came to the fore in the weeks following November 1, 1765, when the Stamp Act went into effect. The strategy of opposition chosen by the colonial leadership was to cease all activities which required the use of stamps. Thus maritime trade came to a halt in the cities. Some said that this was a cowardly strategy. If the Americans opposed the Stamp Act, let them go on with business as usual, refusing outright to use the stamps. The leaders' strategy was especially harmful to the seamen, and the latter took the more radical position—otherwise the ships would not sail. And this time the seamen's radicalism triumphed over both colonial leadership and British officials. Within little more than a month the act had been largely nullified. Customs officers were allowing ships to sail without stamps, offering as the reason the fear that the seamen, "who are the people that are most dangerous on these occasions, as their whole dependance for a subsistence is upon Trade," would certainly "commit some terrible Mischief." Philadelphia's customs officers feared that the seamen would soon "compel" them to let ships pass without stamps. Customs officers at New York yielded when they heard that the seamen were about to have a meeting.

Customs officers had worse luck on the other days. Seamen battled them throughout the 1760's and 1770's. In October 1769 a Philadelphia customs officer was attacked by a mob of seamen who also tarred, feathered, and nearly drowned a man who had furnished him with information about illegally imported goods. A year later a New Jersey customs officer who approached an incoming vessel in Delaware Bay had *his* boat boarded by armed seamen who threatened to murder him and came close to doing so. When the officer's son came to Philadelphia, he was similarly treated by a mob of seamen; there were one thousand seamen in Philadelphia at the time, and according to the customs collector there, they were "always ready" to do such "mischief." This old antagonism had been further politicized in 1768 when, under the American Board of Customs Commissioners, searchers began to break into sea chests and confiscate those items not covered by cockets, thus breaking an old custom of the sea which allowed seamen to import small items for their own profit. Oliver M. Dickerson has described this new "Invasion of Seamen's Rights" as a part of "customs racketeering" and a cause of animosity between seamen and customs officers.

Many of these animosities flared in the Boston Massacre. What John Adams described as "a motley rabble of saucy boys, negroes and mulattoes, Irish teagues and out landish jack tarrs," including twenty or thirty of the latter, armed with clubs and sticks, did battle with the soldiers. Their leader was Crispus Attucks, a mulatto seaman; he was shot to death in front of the Custom House. One of the seamen's reasons for being there has been too little explored. The Massacre grew out of a fight between workers and off-duty soldiers at a ropewalk two days before. That fight, in turn, grew out of the long-standing practice in the British army of allowing off-duty soldiers to take civilian employment. They did so, in Boston and elsewhere, often at wages which undercut those offered to Americans—including unemployed seamen who sought work ashore—by as much as 50 percent. In hard times this led to intense competition for work, and the Boston Massacre was in part a product of this competition. Less well known is the Battle of Golden Hill, which arose from similar causes and took place in New York six weeks before. In January 1770 a gang of seamen went from house to house and from dock to dock, using clubs to drive away the soldiers employed there and threatening anyone who might rehire them. In the days of rioting which followed and which came to be called the Battle of Golden Hill, the only fatality was a seaman, although many other seamen were wounded in the attempt to take vengeance for the killing. The antipathy between soldiers and seamen was so great, said John Adams, "that they fight as naturally when they meet, as the elephant and Rhinoceros."

## IV

To wealthy Loyalist Judge Peter Oliver of Massachusetts, the common people were only "Rabble"—like the "Mobility of all Countries, perfect Machines, wound up by any Hand who might first take the Winch." The people were "duped," "deceived," and "deluded" by cynical leaders who could "turn the Minds of the great Vulgar." Had they been less ignorant, Americans would have spurned their leaders, and there would have been no Revolution. I have tested this generalization and found it unacceptable, at least in its application to colonial seamen. Obviously the seamen did not cause the American Revolution. But neither were they simply irrational fellows who moved only when others manipulated them. I have attempted to show that the seaman had a mind of his own and genuine reasons to act, and that he did act—purposefully. The final test of this purposefulness must be the Revolution itself. Here we find situations in which the seamen are separated from those who might manipulate them and thrown into great physical danger; if they were manipulated or duped into rebellion, on their own we might expect them to show little understanding of or enthusiasm for the war.

To a surprising extent American seamen remained Americans during the Revolution. Beaumarchais heard from an American in 1775 that seamen, fishermen, and harbor workers had become an "army of furious men, whose actions are all animated by a spirit of vengeance and hatred" against the English, who had destroyed their livelihood "and the liberty of their country." The recent study of loyalist claimants by Wallace Brown confirms Oliver Dickerson's earlier contention that "the volumes dealing with loyalists and their claims discloses an amazing absence of names" of seamen. From a total of 2786 loyalist claimants whose occupations are known Brown found only 39, 1.4 percent, who were seamen (or pilots). (It is possible to exclude fishermen and masters but not pilots from his figures.) In contrast, farmers numbered 49.1 percent, artisans 9.8 percent, merchants and shopkeepers 18.6 percent, professionals 9.1 percent, and officeholders 10.1 percent. Although as Brown states, the poor may be underrepresented among the claimants, "the large number of claims by poor people, and even Negroes, suggests that this is not necessarily true."

An especially revealing way of examining the seamen's loyalties under pressure is to follow them into British prisons. Thousands of them were imprisoned in such places as the ship *Jersey*, anchored in New York harbor, and Mill and Forton prisons in England. Conditions were abominable. Administration was corrupt, and in America disease was rife and thousands died. If physical discomfort was less in English prisons than in *Jersey*, the totality of misery may have been as great, with prisoners more distant from the war and worse informed about the progress of the American cause. Lost in a no-man's land between British refusal to consider them prisoners of war and Washington's unwillingness in America to trade trained soldiers for captured seamen, these men had limited opportunities for exchange. Trapped in this very desperate situation, the men were offered a choice: they could defect and join the Royal Navy. To a striking extent the prisoners remained patriots, and very self-consciously so. "Like brave men, they resisted, and swore that they would never lift a hand to do any thing on board of King George's ships." The many who stayed understood the political significance of their choice as well as the few who went. "What business had he to sell his Country, and go to the worst of Enemies?" Instead of defecting they engaged in an active resistance movement. Although inexperienced in self-government and segregated from their captains, on their own these men experienced no great difficulties in organizing themselves into disciplined groups. "Notwithstanding they were located within the absolute dominions of his Britanic majesty," commented one, the men "adventured to form themselves into a republic, framed a constitution and enacted wholesome laws, with suitable penalties." Organized, they resisted, celebrating the Fourth of July under British bayonets, burning their prisons, and escaping. Under these intolerable conditions, seamen from all over the colonies discovered that they shared a common conception of the cause for which they fought.

At the Constitutional Convention Banjamin Franklin spoke for the seamen:

It is of great consequence that we shd. not depress the virtue and public spirit of our common people; of which they displayed a great deal during the war, and which contributed principally to the favorable issue of it. He related the honorable refusal of the American seamen who were carried in great numbers into the British prisons during the war, to redeem themselves from misery or to seek their fortunes, by entering on board of the Ships of the Enemies to their Country; contrasting their patriotism with a contemporary instance in which the British seamen made prisoners by the Americans, readily entered on the ships of the latter on being promised a share of the prizes that might be made out of their own Country.

Franklin spoke *against limiting* the franchise, not *for broadening* it: he praised the seamen, but with a hint of condescension, suggesting that it would be prudent to grant them a few privileges. A decade later a French traveller noticed that "except the laborer in ports, and the common sailor, everyone calls himself, and is called by others, a *gentleman*." Government was still gentlemen's government: more people were defined as gentlemen, but Jack Tar was not yet among them.

## V

Bernard Bailyn has recently added needed illumination to our understanding of pre-Revolutionary crowd action. Bailyn has disagreed with Peter Oliver and with modern historians who have concurred in describing pre-Revolutionary rioters as mindless, passive, and manipulated: "far from being empty vessels," rioters in the decade before the outbreak of fighting were "politically effective" and "shared actively the attitudes and fears" of their leaders; theirs was a "fully-fledged political movement." Thus it would seem that Bailyn has freed himself from the influential grasp of Gustave

Le Bon. But Bailyn stopped short of total rejection. Only in 1765, he says, was the colonial crowd "transformed" into a political phenomenon. Before then it was "conservative"—like crowds in seventeenth- and eighteenth-century England, aiming neither at social revolution nor at social reform, but only at immediate revenge. Impressment riots and other "demonstrations by transient sailors and dock workers," Bailyn says, expressed no "deep-lying social distress" but only a "diffuse and indeliberate antiauthoritarianism"; they were "ideologically inert."

Other historians have seen the colonial seamen—and the rest of the lower class—as mindless and manipulated, both before and after 1765. The seeming implication behind this is that the seamen who demonstrated in colonial streets did so as much out of simple vindictiveness or undisciplined violence as out of love of liberty. Certainly such motivation would blend well with the traditional picture of the seaman as rough and ready. For along with the stereotype of Jolly Jack—and in part belying that stereotype—is bold and reckless Jack, the exotic and violent. Jack *was* violent; the conditions of his existence were violent. Was his violence non-political? Sometimes. The mob of seventy to eighty yelling, club-swinging, out-of-town seamen who tried to break up a Philadelphia election in 1742 had no interest in the election; they had been bought off with money and liquor.

Other violence is not so clear-cut. Edward Thompson has seen the fighting out of significant social conflict in eighteenth-century England "in terms of Tyburn, the hulks and the Bridewells on the one hand, and crime, riot, and mob action on the other." Crime and violence among eighteenth-century American seamen needs reexamination from such a perspective. Does "mutiny" adequately describe the act of the crew which seized *Black Prince*, re-named it *Liberty*, and chose their course and a new captain by voting? What shall we call the conduct of 150 seamen who demanded higher wages by marching along the streets of Philadelphia with clubs, unrigging vessels, and forcing workmen ashore? If "mutiny" is often the captain's name for what we have come to call a "strike," perhaps we might also detect some significance broader than mere criminality in the seamen's frequent assaults on captains and thefts from them. Is it not in some sense a political act for a seaman to tear off the mast a copy of a law which says that disobedient seamen will be punished as "seditious"?

Impressment meant the loss of freedom, both personal and economic, and, sometimes, the loss of life itself. The seaman who defended himself against impressment felt that he was fighting to defend his "liberty," and he justified his resistance on grounds of "right." It is in the concern for liberty and right that the seaman rises from vindictiveness to a somewhat more complex awareness that certain values larger than himself exist and that he is the victim not only of cruelty and hardship but also, in the light of those values, of injustice. The riots ashore, whether they be against impressment, the Stamp Act, or competition for work express that same sense of injustice. And here, thousands of men took positive and effective steps to demonstrate their opposition to both acts and policies.

Two of England's most exciting historians have immensely broadened our knowledge of past and present by examining phenomena strikingly like the conduct and thought of the seamen in America. These historians have described such manifestations as "sub-political" or "pre-political," and one of them has urged that such movements be "seriously considered not simply as an unconnected series of individual curiosities, as footnotes to history, but as a phenomenon of general importance and considerable weight in modern history." When Jack Tar went to sea in the American Revolution, he fought, as he had for many years before, quite literally, to protect his life, liberty, and property. It might be extravagant to call the seamen's conduct and the sense of injustice which underlay it in any fully developed sense ideological or political; on the other hand, it makes little sense to describe their ideological content as zero. There are many worlds and much of human history in that vast area between ideology and inertness.

Chattel Slavery for Blacks

and The Revolution

BENJAMIN QUARLES (b. 1904) has written a number of influential studies on blacks in American history, including *The Negro in the American Revolution*. In this essay, Quarles focuses upon the ramifications of an incident that took place in Revolutionary Virginia when the last royal governor, Lord Dunmore, issued a modified emancipation proclamation in November of 1775, thus threatening to disrupt the Virginia planters' economy and society by encouraging overt black resistance to the spreading rebellion. To Quarles, Dunmore's words were particularly important for the indirect effect they had on thousands of slaves beyond those who rose up in 1775, encouraging them in the hope that eventual freedom through the Revolution was possible. Were the slaves who dared to resist their Virginia masters pursuing a more realistic course of action despite the possibility that they would remain slaves under the British?

# Lord Dunmore as Liberator

In American patriotic tradition the first full-fledged villain to step from the wings as the Revolutionary War unfolded was John Murray, Earl of Dunmore. Like other royal governors in office as the crisis reached its pitch, the Crown's representative in Virginia would have been a marked man no matter how circumspect his behavior. Dunmore, lacking in diplomatic skills, was destined to furnish the colonies with a convenient hate-symbol. The one act that most thoroughly defamed his name was a deed which in Negro circles cast its author in the role of liberator. This was Dunmore's proclamation inviting slaves to leave their masters and join the royal forces.

Issued as of November 7, 1775, on board the *William* in the harbor at Norfolk, the proclamation announced that in order to defeat "treasonable purposes" the governor was establishing martial law. Colonists who refused "to resort to his Majesty's standard" were to be adjusted traitors. Then came the words which were destined to be quoted far and wide: "and I do hereby

From Benjamin Quarles, "Lord Dunmore as Liberator," *William and Mary Quarterly*, 3rd Sers., XV (1958), pp. 494–507. Reprinted by permission of the Institute of Early American History and Culture and the author. Footnotes omitted.

further declare all indented servants, Negroes, or others, (appertaining to Rebels,) free, that are able and willing to bear arms, they joining His Majesty's Troops, as soon as may be, for the more speedily reducing the Colony to a proper sense of their duty, to His Majesty's crown and dignity."

Dunmore's proclamation had its expected effect. "The colonists," wrote a contemporary , "were struck with horror"; the "Poet of the American Revolution" implored the heavens to deliver the colonies from the "valiant" Dunmore and "his crew of banditti" ("who plunder Virginians at Williamsburg city"). Taking alarm, the Continental Congress lost no time in bestirring itself. On December 2, 1775, the delegates instructed the "Committee for fitting our armed vessels" to engage ships of war for the taking or destroying of the governor's fleet, and the presiding officer urged the commander in chief of the Continental Army to take such measures against his lordship as would "effectually Repel his violences and secure the peace and safety of that Colony." Two days later the Congress recommended to Virginia that she resist Dunmore "to the utmost. . . . "

The apprehension over Dunmore's proclamation was gounded primarily in the fear of its unsettling effect on the slaves, if not in the fear of a servile insurrection—that nightmarish dread in communities where the whites were outnumbered. A policy that would strike off their shackles would obviously have a marked appeal to the inhabitants of slave row. Moreover, there had been recent evidence that the Virginia bondmen were responsive to the offer of freedom.

Dunmore himself had furnished such evidence. For at least eight months prior to the formal proclamation, the governor had seriously considered the idea of enlisting the slaves. His reasons were plain. Rebellious planters who contemplated a resort to arms would be deprived of their workers and would be compelled to return to their homes to protect their families and their property. Moreover, the slaves would help fill the ranks of military laborers for His Majesty's forces, and such human *potentiel de guerre* was badly needed. And Dunmore could expect little help from British headquarters in Boston. Obviously, too, the Crown supporters and their sympathizers counted on the disaffection of the Negroes in the South.

Needing supporters to hold the rebellion-bent Virginians in check, Dunmore let it be known late in April 1775 that he might be driven to set up the royal standard, adding that if he did he believed that he could count on "all the Slaves on the side of Government." On May 1 the governor wrote to the Earl of Dartmouth expressing confidence that, once supplied with arms and ammunition, he would be able "to collect from among the *Indians,* negroes and other persons" a force sufficient to hold his own. Two weeks later, Gage in a letter to Dartmouth touched on Dunmore's proposal: "We hear," wrote the British commander, "that a Declaration his Lordship has made, of proclaiming all the Negroes free, who should join him, has Startled the Insurgents."

In late April a group of slaves, scenting freedom in the air, went to the governor's house and volunteered their services, but Dunmore had them dismissed. He was then not quite ready for the open break, but it could not be long delayed. On June 8, 1775, the governor took the decisive step of quitting Williamsburg and taking asylum aboard the man-of-war *Fowey* at Yorktown, a move he had been turning over in his mind since May 15. "I have thought it best for his Majesty's Service," he wrote, "to retire from amidst such hostile appearances around me." The House of Burgesses, taking note of the governor's flight, assured him that his personal safety was in no danger, but pointedly noted its displeasure that "a Scheme, the most diabolical, had been meditated, and generally recommended, by a Person of great Influence, to offer Freedom to our Slaves and turn them against their Masters."

Realizing that there was no turning back, Dunmore initiated a policy of unofficial slave solicitation to augment his tiny force of three hundred white soldiers, seamen, and loyalist recuits. In early August the "Officers of the Volunteer Companies" in Williamsburg informed the Convention that the "Governour's Cutter had carried off a number of Slaves belonging to private gentlemen. . . . " Small sloops, which were employed primarily to intercept intracolonial shipments of powder, invited slaves aboard. "Lord Dunmore sails up and down the river," wrote a Norfolk correspondent on October 28, 1775, to a friend in England, "and where he finds a defenceless place, he lands, plunders the plantation and carries off the negroes."

Now ready to come out into the open, Dunmore was concerned only with his timing. An apparently auspicious moment came in mid-November 1775 when a skirmish took place at Kemp's Landing on the Elizabeth River. In this action the colonial militia was routed and its two commanding colonels were captured. Entering the village in triumph, Dunmore, on November 14, ordered the publication of the proclamation he had drafted a week earlier on board the *William*. The final break had come—the governor had set up his standard and had officially called upon the slaves to join him.

Tidewater Virginia took alarm as rumors spread that the slaves were stampeding to the British. But there were strong deterring factors. Foremost among these was the military alertness of the Virginians themselves. Before any substantial slave migration to Dunmore could get under way, the governor suffered a decisive defeat at arms. This occurred on December 9 at Great Bridge, a fortified span across the Elizabeth River some ten miles below Norfolk which dominated the land approach thereto. Dunmore had believed that an attack was impending and had rashly decided to take the offensive. His force of six hundred was severely repulsed, suffering sixty-one casualties, including three dead officers. Forced to retreat after twenty-five minutes of combat, Dunmore's troops hurried back to Norfolk. Feeling that he could no longer hold the city and fearing a retaliatory attack, the governor spiked his twenty pieces of cannon and ordered his followers aboard the vessels in the harbor. He was never to regain a foothold on the Virginia mainland.

The military preparation of the colonists was matched by their promptness in adopting "home front" measures to prevent slaves from joining the governor. Newspapers lost no time in publishing the proclamation in full, as information and as a warning. To deter runaways local patrol groups were doubled, highways were carefully watched, and owners of small craft were required to exercise vigilance. Since Dunmore's action had come as no surprise, the Virginians had had time to put the colony in a "tolerable state of defense." Adjacent Maryland, through its Council of Safety, ordered the military to station itself, in St. Mary's County "and guard the shores from thence to the river Powtowmack, to prevent any servants, negroes, or others from going on board the Fowey ship of war."

To vigilance the colonists added psychological warfare. In Alexander Purdie's *Virginia Gazette* was published a letter from a subscriber urging that Negroes be cautioned against joining Dunmore. Slaves should be told that the English ministry, in refusing to stop the slave trade, had proved a far greater enemy to Negroes than their American masters, and that if the colonists were defeated, their slaves would be sold to the West Indies. They should be told, too, continued Mr. Purdie's correspondent, that Dunmore was cruel to his own black servitors. And, finally, they should be urged to place their expectation on "a better condition in the next world." If this information had been spread widely, "not one slave would have joined our enemies."

A week later the *Gazette* carried another letter in similar vein. Colonists were advised to inform slaves that Dunmore proposed to free only those who would bear arms for him, leaving the aged and infirm, the women and children, to bear the brunt of the shorn master's anger. Moreover, under the English flag the slaves would be much worse off than under Virginia masters, "who pity their condition, who wish in general to make it as easy and comfortable as possible, and who would willingly, were it in their power, or were they permitted, not only prevent any more negroes from losing their freedom, but restore it to such as have already unhappily lost it." Contrast this with the British, ran the *Gazette's* warning, who would sell the runaways to the sugar islands. "Be not then, ye negroes, tempted by this proclamation to ruin your selves."

Official action was not long in coming. The Virginia Convention on December 8 appointed a committee to prepare an answer to Dunmore's proclamation. Five days later, when the committee made its report, it was directed to draw up a declaration stating that runaways to the British would be pardoned if they returned in ten days; otherwise they would "be liable to such punishment as shall be directed by the Convention." The following day, with the committee's report at hand, the delegates issued a declaration of policy. Beginning with a reminder that the time-honored penalty for a slave insurrection was death without benefit of clergy, the document stated that Negroes who had been "seduced" to take up arms were liable to punishment. But in order that they might return in safety to their duties, they would be pardoned if they laid down their arms forthwith. The proclamation concluded with a request to "all humane and benevolent persons in the colony" to convey to the slaves this "offer of mercy." To insure a wide circulation, the proclamation was published as a broadside.

The Virginians supplemented techniques of persuasion and sweet reasonableness with alternatives more forthright and punitive. In early December the Convention decreed that slaves taken in arms were to be sold to the foreign West Indies, with the sale money, minus expenses, to go to their masters. Somewhat less severe was the fate of captured runaways who had failed in their attempts to reach the King's forces. Such slaves, if their masters were patriots, were returned to their home plantations, often after first serving a term of imprisonment. An owner of a captured runaway might be ordered to "convey him to some interior part of the Country as soon as may be. . . . " Slaves of British sympathizers were put to work in the lead mines, a practice which became customary in Virginia for the duration of the war. Distrusting all Negroes who had joined the governor, the Convention recommended that military officers "seize and secure" even those who came bearing flags of truce.

The death penalty was used sparingly. In Northampton County the court passed such a sentence on a group of thirteen salves who had seized a schooner at Hungers Creek and sailed into the bay, their destination the James. Overtaken by a whale boat, their execution was set for April 2, 1776. But the Northampton Committee of Safety sent word to Williamsburg inquiring whether the punishment should not be mitigated since the seizing of the boat was more "intended to effect an escape to Dunmore than any other Design of committing a felony." When-

ever the death sentence was passed, as in the case of two runaways who mistook an armed vessel of the Virginia navy for a British man-of-war, it was used mainly "as an example to others."

Despite preventive efforts, whether an appeal to common sense or a resort to legal reprisals, many slaves made their way to the British, spurred in part by loyalist propaganda of the governor's good treatment. Some two hundred "immediately joined him," and within a week after the proclamation the number had reached three hundred. "Numbers of Negros and Cowardly Scoundrels flock to his Standard," wrote a member of the provincial Committee of Safety.

Since Dunmore had no base on the mainland after mid-December 1775, the Negroes who sought his sanctuary were water-borne. Two weeks after the proclamation a group of slaves came down the James in a thirty-foot vessel, bound for the fleet off Norfolk, but they were captured near Surry. Shortly afterward seven Negroes broke out of a Northampton jail and "went off in a pettinger," bound for the British ships. Colonel Landon Carter of the Sabine Hall plantation made a diary notation of the break for the open water executed by ten of his retainers:

26 Wednesday, June, 1776. Last night after going to bed, Moses, my son's man, Joe, Billy, Postillion, John, Mullatto Peter, Tom, Panticove, Manuel & Lancaster Sam, ran away, to be sure, to Ld. Dunmore, for they got privately into Beale's room before dark & took out my son's gun & one I had there, took out of his drawer in my passage all his ammunition furniture, Landon's bag of bullets and all the Powder, and went off in my Petty Auger [pettiauger] new trimmed, and

it is supposed that Mr. Robinson's People are gone with them, for a skow they came down in is, it seems, at my Landing. These accursed villians have stolen Landon's silver buckles, George's shirts, Tom Parker's new waistcoat & breeches.

The Negroes who reached the British were generally able-bodied men who could be put to many uses. It was as soldiers, however, that Dunmore envisioned them, and he enlisted them from the beginning. By early December he was arming them "as fast as they came in." He made use of Negro privates at the rout of the colonials at Kemp's Landing; indeed, slaves had captured one of the two commanding colonels. In the skirmishes preceding the action at Great Bridge, two runaways who were taken prisoner testified that the garrison was manned by thirty whites and ninety Negroes, and that "all the blacks who are sent to the fort at the great Bridge, are supplied with muskets, Cartridges & strictly ordered to use them defensively & offensively." By the first of December the British had nearly three hundred slaves outfitted in military garb, with the inscription, "Liberty to Slaves," emblazoned across the breast of each. The governor officially designated them "Lord Dunmore's Ethiopian Regiment."

The first and only major military action in which Dunmore's forces were engaged was the Battle of Great Bridge. Of the governor's troops of some six hundred men, nearly half were Negroes. Of the eighteen wounded prisoners taken by the Virginians in this route, two were former slaves. James Anderson was wounded "in the Forearm—Bones shattered and flesh much torn," and Casar was hit "in the Thigh,

by a Ball, and 5 shot—one lodged." After the fiasco at Great Bridge, the governor was forced to operate from his ships. Taking aboard the hardiest of his Negro followers and placing them under officers who exercised them at small arms, he sanguinely awaited recruits.

Dunmore's use of Negroes also embraced sailoring services. On the six tenders sent by the governor to cannonade Hampton in late October 1775, there were colored crewmen. Two of them were captured when the Virginians seized the pilot boat *Hawk Tender*. To man the small craft that scurried in and out of the river settlements, harassing the plantations, the British depended largely on ex-slaves. Particularly were they needed as pilots. Joseph Harris, a runaway, served as pilot of the *Otter*, having come to Captain Matthew Squire with the highest recommendation from a fellow naval officer. "I think him too useful to His Majesty's service to take away," wrote the latter, because of "his being well acquainted with many creeks in the *Eastern* Shore, at *York*, *James* River, and *Nansemond*, and many others, . . . " and "accustomed to pilot. . . . " Two citizens on the Isle of Wight advised the chairman of the Virginia Committee of Safety to go slow on discharging "a Negro fello, named Caesar," who was not only "a very great Scoundrel" but was also "a fello' they can't do well without being an Excellent pilot."

Another service performed by Dunmore's black followers was foraging. The governor's supply of provisions, particularly fresh food, needed constant replenishing, and the Virginia leaders understandably would not permit the British to send men ashore to make purchases. "Back settlers" who might have been willing to supply his lordship with provisions had "no means of conveying them," and Dunmore was driven to a dependence upon the foraging abilities of his Negro recruits. Marauding parties of predominantly ex-slave composition preyed on the countryside, making a night descent upon a plantation and making off with the choice livestock. One foraging party, captured while on its way to the Eastern Shore, was made up of "one white and sixteen blacks."

Allegedly one of the services of Negroes to Dunmore was germ spreading. That the charge of germ warfare was propaganda-laden did not make it less potent in arousing indignation. The accusation was that Dunmore had inoculated two Negroes and sent them ashore at Norfolk to spread the smallpox. The charge was ironic in view of the fate of the Negroes who fled to the British. The majority of them were disease fatalities. Late in March the governor informed his superior in England that the recruiting of the black regiment "would have been in great forwardness had not a fever crept in amongst them, which carried off a great many very fine fellows." He added that on advice of "medical people here," he had concluded that the trouble came from the overcrowded condition on the ships and the lack of clothing, both of which "we have now provided against."

But the plague persisted, killing off the Negroes and the hope of the governor alike. Writing to Germain in June, Dunmore confessed defeat. The fever, he explained, was malignant, and had "carried off an incredible number of our people, especially blacks." Had this not happened he would have enlisted two thousand Negro followers. He was, ran his letter, separating the sick from the well and would try to keep the two groups from intermingling. The governor's efforts were unavailing; by early June 1776 there were not more than "150 effective Negro men," although each day the black corps was augmented by from six to eight arrivals.

The failure to arrest the smallpox, and the harassment by the Virginia and Maryland militia, finally brought an end to his lordship's stay in Chesapeake waters. In May 1776, faced with the likelihood "of a great reduction of our force" due to disease, the fleet moved from their exposed quarters at Tucker's Mills near Portsmouth and took shelter on Gwynn's Island near the mouth of the Rappahannock. Nowhere were Dunmore and his "floating Town" allowed peace; "we no sooner appear off the land, than signals are made from it," wrote Dunmore to Whitehall, "and if we come to anchor within cannonshot of either shore, guns are immediately brought to bear upon us. . . . "

Early in July the British, after suffering an attack on their shipping, took refuge on St. George's Island in the Potomac. By the end of the month the disease-ridden corps, lacking suitable drinking water, and despairing of re-enforcements, prepared to make their exit. Dismantling, burning, or running aground sixty-three out of their 103 vessels, they sailed out of the Potomac on August 6, seven of the ships bound for Sandy Hook and the others setting a southward course for St. Augustine and the Bermudas. With the departing fleet went some three hundred Negroes, the healthiest going northward, destined for further military service, and Dunmore's schemes came to an inglorious end.

Perhaps not more than a total of eight hundred slaves had succeeded in reaching the British, and perhaps one eighth of these had been brought by loyalist masters. But Dunmore's proclamation undoubtedly had an indirect effect on thousands of additional slaves quickening their hopes for freedom. Perhaps the imagination of colonial editors was behind such stories as that of a colored mother in New York naming her child after his lordship, and that of a Negro in Philadelphia jostling whites on the streets and telling them to wait until "lord Dunmore and his black regiment come, and then we will see who is to take the wall." But whether fact or fabrication, such reports reflect the attitude of expectation that Dunmore engendered among persons of color along the Chesapeake.

It made no difference that he had offered freedom to the bondmen of his enemies only, and that as governor he had withheld his signature from a bill against the slave trade; to those who whispered his name in slave quarters he was in truth the "African Hero" he was derisively dubbed by a Virginia patriot.

If Dunmore was viewed by one group as a tyrant and by another as a liberator, this was but another paradox in a war that abounded in paradox, and another illustration of the war as a social revolution. The Negro who fled to the governor was actuated by the same love of freedom for which the colonists avowedly broke with the mother country. Dunmore's invitation to the slaves was to prefigure the thousands of runaways below the Mason-Dixon line who served as military laborers to His Majesty's forces during the Revolution and who, when peace came, sailed with them from Savannah, Charleston, and New York.

WINTHROP D. JORDAN (b. 1931) has focused his research on early American racial attitudes. In this selection from *White Over Black: American Attitudes toward the Negro, 1550-1812*, Jordan investigates modifications in thoughts and ideas during the Revolutionary years and explores the increasingly important strain of Enlightenment environmentalism. From his evidence, the debate and changes in ideas had more long-range impact upon society and the plight of blacks than did the limited accomplishments against discriminatory and prejudicial practices. In spite of the continued existence of the "peculiar institution," the Revolution mandated that Americans confront the contradiction between the words of liberty and the reality of chattel slavery. Why did the Revolutionaries fail to close that gap? Why did the Revolution not extend to real victims of oppression? Was the debate as important as Jordan claims or did it only side-track the fundamental issue of emancipation?

# Self-Scrutiny
# in the Revolutionary Era

The growth of American self-awareness formed an important theme during the gathering political crisis prior to the Revolution. Indeed the Revolution has been said to have been primarily a revolution in American consciousness. If this was the case in the realm of politics, it was even more so in the shadowy realm of communal intellect and self-identification. But it is impossible to separate completely the two realms, and their inseparability becomes apparent in the development of antislavery during the Revolutionary era. Indeed the assumption of heightening self-awareness in America serves to tie together apparently disparate developments in the period. Americans came to realize that they were no longer Englishmen, at the same time they grew conscious of their own "prejudices" concerning Negroes. As they began to question slavery, they began to see that there was a race problem

From Winthrop D. Jordan, *White Over Black: American Attitudes toward the Negro, 1550-1812*. The University of North Carolina Press, 1968, for the Institute of Early American History and Culture. Reprinted by permission of the publisher. Footnotes omitted.

in America and that it was necessary to assert the fundamental equality of Negroes with white men and to combat suggestions to the contrary. . . .

Amidst the protests against British encroachments upon their liberties in the 1760's and 1770's, some Americans came to realize, in far sharper terms than ever before, that they had on their hands a color problem. At first, despite Woolman's formulation of the problem, recognition came haltingly in the form of ridicule or indignant denial that blackness was any justification for slavery. This line of argument had been advanced long before by proponents of Negro conversion, but ironically and perhaps appropriately, it was first advanced in connection with slavery by a European. The colonists picked up Montesquieu's remarks in the *Spirit of the Laws* (1748) and passed them around the increasingly active antislavery circuit. Erratic young James Otis, delivering one of the opening barrages in defense of colonial rights in 1764, derided the logic of slavery based on color: "The Colonists are by the law of nature free born, as indeed all men are, white or black. No better reasons can be given, for enslaving those of any color than such as baron Montesquieu has humorously given. . . . Does it follow that this right to enslave a man because he is black? Will short curl'd hair like wool, instead of christian hair, as tis called by those, whose hearts are as hard as the nether millstone, help the argument? Can any logical inference in favour of slavery, be drawn from a flat nose, a long or a short face." Antislavery writers took up the theme and played it vigorously. One conjectured that some oppressors of the Negro "perhaps may conceive from their colour that they are of an inferiour species and that they may be oppressed without guilt." Another mocked the claim of the slaveholder: "But they are black, and ought to obey; we are white and ought to rule." A third declared that "Some have been so grossly stupid as to assign colour as a mark for servitude. This, if it could prove any thing would prove too much. It would establish it, that all complexions but the fairest should be, in some degree deprived of liberty. That all black persons should be slaves, says Montesquieu, is as ridiculous as that law of a certain country, that all red-haired persons should be hanged."

Taken at face value, these statements seem to be only slightly more explicit versions of previous assertions of the irrelevance of color to men's proper spiritual condition. The staying power of traditional Christian equalitarianism was evident in admonitions given by the Reverend Andrew Eliot in 1774. "We are all children of the same Father," he insisted; "one God hath created us and he hath, in the essential part of our constitution, fashioned our souls alike. We ought, therefore, to treat one another as brethren. This we may do, and yet a suitable distinction be preserved.—The meanest slave hath a soul as good by nature as your's, and possibly by grace it is better. A dark complection may cover a fair and beautiful mind." What was new about this line of argument was that it achieved wide currency in an atmosphere where slavery seemed not merely wrong but at variance with American professions of attachment to liberty. The logic of color seemed to run counter to the logic of English liberties. If this wedge of an argument were driven very far home, however, it was bound to split open and expose the fundamental problem: extending liberty to Negroes was enormously difficult simply because they did not look like other Americans. As anti-slavery advocates hammered away, the popular assignment of "the colour as a mark for servitude" was bound to become not only "grossly stupid" but a major impediment to emancipation. What was at first perceived as a logical absurdity was gradually recognized to be the rock upon which slavery was founded. . . .

### Assertions of Sameness

The eyes of antislavery advocates tended to fall, therefore, upon problems which were sensed to be more tractable than the Negro's complexion. With the institution of slavery being brought into question by Revolutionary ideology, moreover, antislavery writers were canvassing about for effective arguments in favor of abolition. Though they could not easily defend the Negro's color, they found that they could—and had to—defend his character. They discovered many discreditable human qualities which were associated with Negroes by the "prejudices" of the popular mind, but if Negroes were "brutish, ignorant, idle, crafty, treacherous, bloody, thievish, mistrustful, and superstitious," perhaps they might be reformed. Better still, these unlovely characteristics in the Negro afforded standing arguments for his emancipation. What better way to reform a man than to free him from the bondage of chattel slavery? Escape from the bondage of sin into the liberty of the Christian had always worked

wonders. The logic was particularly effective in that it completely inverted a major justification for slavery: the Negro's immorality and ignorance could be completely transformed by saying that these qualities were not a reason for but the result of enslavement. If the Negro's failings resulted from the very nature of oppression, then all that was required was that oppression be brought to an end. Reform would follow.

Inversion of the causal sequence of vice and slavery was easily accomplished. Dr. Benjamin Rush didactically explained the proper relation between the two conditions: "Slavery is so foreign to the human mind, that the moral faculties, as well as those of the understanding are debased, and rendered torpid by it. All the vices which are charged upon the Negroes in the southern colonies and the West-Indies, such as Idleness, Treachery, Theft, and the like, are the genuine offspring of slavery, and serve as an argument to prove that they were not intended, by Providence for it." William Dillwyn, a perceptive Quaker from Burlington, elaborated this inversion in a private letter: "If the Negroes are generally *unprincipled and vicious*,'" Dillwyn asked (apparently quoting a Dr. Chandler), "is it not the natural Consequence of a State of Slavery? Can we reasonably expect their Morals or Manners will equal those of Freemen, until they are cultivated with the same Degree of Care, in an equally extensive Field of Action, and with the same Encouragement? Were a Number of *Whites* treated just as they are . . . who will venture to assert that it would not occasion a like Depression of Spirit, and consequent Depravity of Manners?" By this reasoning, abolition of slavery was a kindness, a duty, and an impressive act of reformation. . . .

Equalitarian antislavery advocates were so anxious to find tangible evidence for their contentions concerning mental equality that they almost trampled each other in rushing to acclaim the first exemplar of Negro literary talent. A French official living in America during the war took surprised and rather bemused note of the sudden appearance of this remarkable prodigy, "one of the strangest creatures in the country and perhaps in the ·whole world." "Phyllis is a negress," wrote the Marquis de Barbé-Marbois, "born in Africa, brought to Boston at the age of ten, and sold to a citizen of that city. She learned English with unusual ease, eagerly read and reread the Bible, the only book which had been put in her hands, became steeped in the poetic images of which it is full, and at the age of seventeen published a number of poems in which there is imagination, poetry, and zeal, though no correctness nor order nor interest. I read them with some surprise. They are printed, and in the front of the book there are certificates of authenticity which leave no doubt that she is its author." The poems were indeed by Phyllis Wheatley and were first published in London in 1773. The publication of five editions before 1800 and their widespread circulation testified to the importance of the author's race. The poems themselves were written in the effusive, coupleted style so popular in the eighteenth century. One, for example, descanted "On the Death of the Rev. Mr. George Whitefield. 1770."

Hail, happy saint, on thine immortal throne,
Possest of Glory, life, and bliss unknown;
We hear no more the music of thy tongue,
Thy wonted auditories cease to throng.
Thy sermons in unequall'd accents flow'd,
And ev'ry bosom with devotion glow'd;
Thou didst in strains of eloquence refin'd
Inflame the heart, and captivate the mind.
Unhappy we the setting sun deplore,
So Glorious once, but ah! it shines no more.

If lines like these are not well suited to modern tastes, their appearance admirably suited the needs of antislavery advocates. Phillis Wheatley could scarcely have been better for their purposes. She was young, raised in Africe, enslaved, untutored, and a girl to boot. If a Negro laboring under this load of disabilities could write such acceptable poems, how much greater genius might someday be expected to appear among "the sable generation." Phillis Wheatley, "the negro poetess," became antislavery's most prized exhibit; her name virtually a household term for the Negro's mental equality. In far-off Goettingen, Blumenbach triumphantly proclaimed her poems "a collection which scarcely any one who has any taste for poetry could read without pleasure."

The handful of public opponents of Negro equality were disgusted by this lionizing. One of them twitted Benjamin Rush for peddling "a single example of a negro girl writing a few silly poems, to prove that the blacks are not deficient to us in understanding." Bernard Romans, a capable but unorthodox natural philosopher, claimed that "against the Phillis of Boston (who is the *Phaenix* of her race) i could bring at least twenty well known instances of the contrary effect of education on this sable generation." Edward Long, a judge who resided in

Jamaica for a dozen years before returning to England, ridiculed the popular favor accorded these Negro achievements:

What woeful stuff this madrigal would be
In some starv'd, hackney sonneteer, or me!
But let a *Negro* own the happy lines,
How the wit brightens! How the Style refines!
Before his sacred name flies ev'ry fault,
And each exalted stanza teems with thought!

From the very first, Negro literature was chained to the issue of racial equality.

Proponents of Negro equality could scarcely rest their entire case on the poems of a little Negro girl. No matter how successful they were in demonstrating that talent could blossom amidst the weeds of slavery, moreover, equalitarians faced the task of explaining away the embarassingly barbarous condition of unenslaved Negroes in Africa. If the Negro was naturally the equal of the white man, why was he so notoriously barbarous in his natural state? Happily for the antislavery people, there were several routes around this difficulty. Some writers, notably Anthony Benezet, pooh-poohed the alleged barbarism of the Africans. Eagerly thumbing through reports by European travelers in West |Africa, they managed sometimes to portray the life of Negroes unmolested by European travelers in West Africa, This Eden-like picture afforded the further advantage of enabling the writer to entail upon the slave trade all the current manifestations of barbarity in Africa. Thus, a dual purpose was served: the trade stood condemned as responsible for barbaric tribal warfare and enslavement, and the Negroes became the innocent victims of European brutality. It had to be admitted that Africans were at a different stage of civilization, but antislavery advocates announced that they were no more savage than the "Ancient *Britains*" had been before their translation into their undeniably preferable present state. The natives of Africa, furthermore, had never been exposed to the inestimably civilizing influence of Christianity, though no one was able to explain precisely why.

One of the surest reliances for the antislavery people was the African climate; it was easy to fall back on the time-worn principle of Western anthropology that climate made the man. This argument from natural environment was a highly versatile means of conveying the principle of Negro equality, since it could be steered in any direction. It could be easily utilized to confirm the innocence of the African natives in the face of rapacious slave traders: "the Africans are an harmless people," wrote Nathaniel Appleton, "having never gone beyond their own bounds, to trouble mankind; and but for the interruption from white people might enjoy all the sweets of a rural life; being bless'd with a fine fruitful soil, which yields with small labour all the necessaries of life." In similar fashion, it could be used to explain away African barbarism. Did the natives of Africa enslave each other? Excessive heat had depraved them. Did the natives live in ease and peaceful indolence? Their tropical surroundings made exertion unnecessary, since nature readily yielded up its fruits without the strenuous human exertions required in colder climates.

More than anyone, Benjamin Rush, a benevolent physician and a firm patriot, rode the crest of this argument toward the goal of fundamental equality. "I shall allow," he wrote disarmingly in 1773, "that many of them are inferior in Virtue, Knowledge, and the love of Liberty to the Inhabitants of other parts of the World: but this may be explained from *Physical* causes." The vast and forbidding expanses of uninhabited territory which separated the various African nations, Rush continued, had prevented stimulating conquests and the erection of great empires; thus the arts of civilization had been stunted. "The Heat of the Climate in Africa," Rush continued, "by bringing on Indolence of Mind, and Body, exposes them at all Times to Slavery, while the Fertility of the Soil renders the Want of Liberty a less Evil to them, than it is to the Inhabitants of Northern, or less Warm and fruitful Countries." Rush drew himself up for a sweeping summary: "Human Nature is the same in all Ages and Countries; and all the difference we perceive in its Characters in respect to Virtue and Vice, Knowledge and Ignorance, may be accounted for from Climate, Country, Degrees of Civilization, form of Government, or other accidental causes." Writing in 1773 as the eye of the Revolutionary storm passed overhead, Rush epitomized the newly intense concentration of Americans upon their environment.

## Environmentalism and Revolutionary Ideology

No line of reasoning—one might almost say no expression of faith—could have better typified the changed pattern of thought in the Revolutionary era. Indeed, the flowering of environmentalism was one of the major historical developments of the second half of the eighteenth century. It did not of course appear out of nowhere, but because environmentalism was not an idea but a way of thinking it is difficult to trace its development. Certainly the notion that men were powerfully molded by their surroundings was intertwined with other important, long-term trends of thought. Perhaps most important of all was the gradual decomposition of old religious beliefs. Traditionally, the soul of man had to be transformed, not his surroundings. As men paid less attention to the inner drama of salvation, they paid more to their earthly stage. Perhaps the most important intellectual support was provided by John Locke's psychology, which denied the existence of innate ideas and rendered man's mind utterly dependent on sensations of the external world received through the senses. And it seems clear that development of an environmentalist outlook was hastened by the discoveries of savage peoples in the far reaches of the world. For if savage and heathen men were men at all, they simply had to possess capacity for improvement. To assume that savages could be nothing but savage forever implied that God had created some men basically different from others—which was not a possibility. The same discoveries helped impart a naturalistic cast to environmentalism. The axiomatic fact that human beings belonged to a single natural species created by God necessitated the assumption that variations within the species derived from some less august sponsorship. Men seemed to vary by locale. What was more natural than for European intellectuals to scan the peculiar natural features of various localities for clues to the variability of man? Certainly during the eighteenth century both the corruptions and virtues in men had come to look less like rigid functions of their immutable nature and more like elicited responses to their "situation." This view did not presuppose a pervasive goodness in man merely awaiting to be unfettered by a more beneficent environment: human nature still usually seemed dangerously corrupt. It was not malleable; it was an unstable constant, in the sense that human beings possessed enormous potentialities for both egregiously barbarous and admirably civilized behavior. Man's environment functioned, then, as a stimulus to performance—what kind of performance would depend on the environment.

Environmentalism was especially attractive to Americans in the Revolutionary era for a number of reasons. They had always lived in close dependence upon America's natural advantages. In 1760 a people awakening to the inestimable advantages of living on a vast and virgin continent (now providentially cleared, to the north and west, of foreign control) were bound to delight in their surroundings. Then, as the political crisis mounted, they developed a more pressing interest in their habitat. Since they thought of themselves as colonial Englishmen and yet were undergoing an unwelcome estrangement from England, they were compelled to ask what made the child different from the parent, the New World different from the Old, the continent different from the island.

As the Revolutionary logic unfolded, as Americans talked increasingly of the rights of "man"—natural rights—they were impelled to take an environmentalist approach to the differences among men. For if all men everywhere possessed the same rights and were in this sense really created equal, then distinctions among groups of men stood in another category—created not by the Creator but by "accidental causes." After the formal break with England, moreover, the logic of governmental reconstruction and reform required the assumption that men were affected by their political social environment. And environmentalism tended to feed on itself. Once men found that one aspect of their environment, such as "oppression," or "room," or "heat," affected man's behavior, they were the more inclined to scrutinize their surroundings for evidence of other external influences.

The environmentalist mode of thought presupposed that the differences among men were circumstantial, that they were alterable, and that the core of human nature was everywhere, as Benjamin Rush put it, "the same." This postulation of quintessential human nature formed the critical point of contact between environmentalist thinking and the political ideology of the Revolution. Of course the tendency to universalize men into "man" was not new in American political thought when it flowered into the eloquence of 1776. The concept of natural rights belonging to all who were by nature men had been superbly set forth by John Locke and by lesser successors well known to Americans. The concept served admirably to justify revolution. Locke's principles and the Glorious Revolution of 1688–89 itself served as the lodestar of American political thought when colonials began resistance to unpopular imperial measures. From the "liberties of Englishmen" it was an easy step to the universalist asertion that all men had a right to be free.

Natural rights theory argued strongly for an end to Negro slavery, and environmentalist antislavery was closely linked with the political philosophy which carried forward the Revolution. It was inevitable that when mankind was being described as naturally free and equal some men should think of the Negro's condition. Negroes were, as Anthony Benezet put it, "as free as we are by nature." This widely shared presumption led inescapably to realization that Americans were indulging in a monstrous inconsistency. While Americans were claiming liberty for themselves they were denying it to a group of men in their midst. Hundreds of times the appalling gap between word and deed was called to the public's attention. In newspapers and pamphlets of the Revolutionary era, the charge was leveled with vehemence and telling accuracy. "How suits it with the glorious cause of Liberty," asked a correspondent to a Philadelphia newspaper in 1768, "to keep your fellow men in bondage, men equally the work of your great Creator, men formed for freedom as yourselves." A New Jersey man wrote in 1780 that "if after we have made a declaration to the world, we continue to hold our fellow creatures in slavery, our words must rise up in judgement against us, and by the breath of our own mouths we shall stand condemned." Even before the Declaration of Independence anti-slavery advocates were crying out the theme of inconsistency.

Blush ye pretended votaries for freedom! ye trifling patriots! who are making a vain parade of being advocates for the liberties of mankind, who are thus making a mockery of your profession by trampling on the sacred rights and privileges of Africans; for while you are fasting, praying, nonimporting, nonexporting, remonstrating, resolving, and pleading for a restoration of your charter rights, you at the same time are continuing this lawless, cruel, inhuman, and abominable practice of enslaving your fellow creatures. . . .

At one level, these protests against slavery merely projected American colonial liberties onto all men, including Negroes. The preamble of a Rhode Island law (1774) prohibiting slave importation noted simply: "Whereas, the inhabitants of America are generally engaged in the preservation of their own rights and liberties, among which, that of personal freedom must be considered as the greatest: as those who are desirous of enjoying all the advantages of liberty themselves, should be willing to extend personal liberty to others." At a more dynamic level of logic, however, the semantics of Revolutionary protest gave special power to the argument from freedom for American colonials to freedom for Negroes. From the beginning of the Revolutionary agitation, the colonists had cried that ministerial tyranny tended to make "slaves" of freeborn Englishmen. This common contention that they were being reduced to a state of "slavery" was more than hyperbole; many colonists believed wholeheartedly that there was a conspiracy on foot to deprive them of their liberties. Nor was this belief entirely the child of radical paranoia in New England. George Washington wrote in 1774, "the crisis is arrived when we must assert our rights, or submit to every imposition, that can be heaped upon us, till custom and use shall make us tame and abject slaves, as the blacks we rule over with such arbitrary sway." Because Revolutionary fervor was pitted against this deprivation—which was "slavery"—it was the more easily transferred to the Negro's condition, which had long borne that now odious name. The Revolutionary struggle was hitched to the struggle against Negro slavery by a stout semantic link. . . .

### The Proslavery Case for Negro Inferiority

Proslavery writers were for the most part unwilling or unable or afraid to challenge the philosophy of equal rights directly. One way to avoid doing so was to assert that the Negro was not the white man's equal. The most extreme attempt of this sort was by the anonymous author of *Personal Slavery Established,* published in the midst of a pamphlet debate over slavery in Philadelphia in 1773. Certain possibilities inhering in a naturalistic view of man became abundantly clear as he effortlessly wrote off the Negro's humanity merely by manipulating Linnaean categories. Of the species known as man, he wrote with caustic condescension, Africans were actually "*species* of that *genus*, though utterly devoid of reason." He went on to "subdivide the Africans into five *classes*, arranging them in the order as they approach nearest to reason, as 1st, Negroes, 2nd, Ourang Outangs, 3rd, Apes, 4th, Baboons, and 5th, Monkeys. The opinion of their irrationality is so well supported by *facts*, that to those acquainted with them, I need

advance very little on the subject." Here was hierarchic classification with a vengeance. Amid controversy over slavery in America, two streams of scientific thought found their confluence. This unknown author took up the element of hierarchy in the Great Chain of Being and stamped it with the rigid specificity of Linnaean classification. Linnaeus would have been appalled had he ever looked upon this powerful engine of oppression.

Less dramatically but no less significantly, virtually all the writers intent on degrading the Negro became enmeshed in the logical thicket of environmentalism. With antislavery advocates laying all the Negro's admitted unattractive characteristics at the door of slavery or to the climate and mode of living in Africa, these frustrated writers could only protest that these characteristics were "natural" to Negroes. In doing so they helped to sharpen, just as the antislavery writers did, the concept of innate as opposed to acquired qualities in man. Refuting the environmentalist assertions of Negro equality, however, was rather like spearing an army of ants with a toothpick, since the Negro's environment was not one influence but thousands. Bernard Romans plainly came off second best when he declared in 1775, "Treachery, theft, stubbornness, and idleness . . . are such consequences of their manner of life at home [in Africa] as to put it out of all doubt that these qualities are natural to them and not originated by their state of slavery." The Negro's "manner of life" in Africa had long since been claimed by the antislavery people as a portion of his environment.

One indication of the slippery strength of the environmentalist argument was the frustrated hyperbole of its opponents. The author of *Personal Slavery Established* plagiarized David Hume in order to combat the environmentalist contentions of Benjamin Rush. "There never was a civilized nation of any other complexion than *white*; nor ever any individual eminent either in action or speculation that was not rather inclining to the *fair*. Africa, except a small part of it, inhabited by those of our own colour, is totally overrun with Barbarism." Having reassured his readers that "the Europeans are blessed with reason, and therefore capable of improvement," he denied Rush's contention that Negroes possessed "genius." He was willing to admit their "docility," though, in "a few such instances" as West Indian Negro craftsmen and one remarkable fellow who could handle double-entry bookkeeping. A "mere *Lusus Naturae*," however, was no evidence" of their being endued with reason." Everyone knew that "extraordinary instances of docility in brutes have naturally excited great admiration in all ages." Pliny, indeed, had described an African elephant who carried on the tinker's trade "with some reputation." The author concluded by baiting the antislavery writers with remarks about provisioning the West Indian islands with the bodies of slaves ("cured in pickle or smoak") who died on route from Africa or in the islands. "A considerable quantity of provision might be thus procured that would furnish a tolerable succedaneum for *pork* and hams." Fortunately no one bothered to reply.

A far more effective tactic against the logic of environmentalism was to stay within the realm of known "facts" about the Negro and then to deal with the *probabilities* concerning his inherent nature. Richard Nisbet, an emotionally unstable West Indian living in Pennsylvania who later turned to the Negro's defense and closed his life in tragic insanity, undertook this task when assailing Benjamin Rush in 1773. "It is impossible to determine, with accuracy," Nisbet wrote, "whether their intellects or ours are superior, as individuals, no doubt, have not the same opportunities of improving as we have." Having thus disarmed the environmentalists by admitting the validity of their first principles, Nisbet went on to appeal to evidence which is still used today for the same purpose. "However, on the whole," he wrote with becoming moderation, "it seems probable, that they are a much inferior race of men to the whites, in every respect. We have no other method of judging, but by considering their genius and government in their native country. Africa, except the small part of it inhabited by those of our own colour, is totally over-run with barbarism." With a nod to David Hume, Nisbet plunged down the usual list of defects —the absence of great kingdoms, the despotism, the lack of any ideas concerning a supreme Being, the hopeless deficiency of friendship and gratitude. Africans, in short, were "utterly unacquainted with the arts, letters, manufactures, and every thing which constitutes civilized life. . . . A few instances may be found, of African negroes possessing virtues and becoming ingenius: but still, what I have said, with regard to their general character. I dare say, most people acquainted with them, will agree to." Nisbet's tract came closer than anyone's to joining the debate with the equalitarians. American antislavery advocates felt confident, however, in relying upon the power they saw in environmental influences; they remained certain that the equality of Negroes prescribed by benevolence, the natural rights philosophy, and the injunctions of religion would eventually be confirmed in actuality by appropriate alterations in the Negro's environment. Detailed exegesis of Scripture, so natural to Samuel Sewall, no longer seemed relevant to the main issue. The flurry of public discussion of slavery in 1773 in Philadelphia was capped by a piece in the *Pennsylvania Packet* which pretended to find in Genesis a passage indicating that Adam and his posterity had been granted dominion not only over fish, fowl, cattle, and all creeping things, "but likewise in a particular manner over the negroes of Africa." The cited passage was, indeed, most explicit: "And the beasts of Æthiopia shall bow down to thee, even they whose figure and speech are like onto thine own, and whose heads are covered like unto fine wool. They who dwell on the sea coast, shall serve thee, and thy seed after thee, even they who shall sojourn in the Islands afar off, where the sun hath his going down." Certainly this was a new way of bringing Scripture to bear on Negro slavery. One turgid debate over slavery in the *Connecticut Journal*, probably stimulated by the pamphlet warfare of 1773 in Philadelphia, did indeed revolve dizzily around genuine chapter and verse, but both parties become bogged down in intricacies which, even in Connecti-

cut, no longer held much fascination. All that the anonymous proslavery writer had to say about Negroes as such was that they were descended from Ham and were "a race of men devoted to slavery."

Many Americans were more alive to the real issues. At Harvard commencement in 1773 two students formally debating "The Legality of Enslaving the Africans" touched upon most of them. Both agreed that Negroes were "brethren" to the whites. The proslavery speaker declaimed that the "real character" of the Africans appeared to be a compound of "a child, an ideot," and "a madman." His opponent was at considerable pains to refute the charge of hopeless barbarism in Africa and to deprecate recent attempts to prove Negroes a different species. As yet, however, the antislavery people were not fully alive to the dangerous flanking movement represented by the utilization of the Great Chain of Being in *Personal Slavery Established.*

### The Revolution as Turning Point

What is particularly impressive about the debate over the Negro's nature during the Revolutionary period is how much the fundamental issue of nature versus nurture had crystallized and yet at the same time how far removed it still was from its modern form. The increased self-consciousness about human behavior which characterized the period greatly sharpened men's sense of the dichotomy between themselves and their social and natural surroundings. With varying degrees of perceptiveness, the equalitarians utilized—and thereby reinforced—this dichotomy, and at the same time dimly recognized its dangers. For if environment was rigidly separated from innate nature, proponents of slavery could as easily grasp one as antislavery people the other. The risks involved in dueling with these weapons were not, of course, so apparent to equalitarians as they were later to become. Though as early as 1762 Anthony Benezet could quote an English antislavery advocate as protesting that men dealing in slaves possessed "a Kind of confused Imagination, or half formed Thought, in their Minds, that the *Blacks* are hardly of the same Species with the white Men, but are Creatures of a Kind somewhat inferior," as late as 1784 James Ramsay, a prominent English opponent of slavery, thought it safe to conjecture that if "negroes are an inferior race; it is a conclusion that hitherto has lain hid and unobserved, and while it leads only to an abuse of power in the superior race, it is better concealed, than drawn out into notice. Perhaps Providence may keep it doubtful, till men be so far improved, as not to make an ill use of the discovery." Just how ill a use some men could make of such a discovery Ramsay was to discover very shortly.

Nothing could illustrate more clearly the transitional character of Revolutionary thought on the question of Negro inferiority than the remarks of Arthur Lee. While studying in Edinburgh in 1764 the petulant young Virginian undertook an anonymous defense of the American colonists against Adam Smith, who had pointedly criticized the practice of slaveholding. Lee hated British criticism, but since he also hated slavery the only way he could get at Smith was to attack Smith's laudatory estimate of Negroes, drawing upon the Churchills' *Voyages* for ammunition. With volcanic energy Lee spewed forth a tirade of condemnation: African characteristics were "cruelty, cunning, perfidy, and cowardice"; their feeding habits were like those of "absolute brutes"; their religion was "the most gross idolatry," which entirely suited "the universal depravity and barbarism of their natures." As Lee summarized his exhaustive roster of depravities, "We have seen that this his [Smith's] nation of heroes is a race the most detestable and vile that ever the earth produced. . . . Aristotle, long ago, declared, that slaves could have no virtue; but he knew not any who were so utterly devoid of any semblance of virtue as are the Africans; whose understandings are generally shallow, and their hearts cruel, vindictive, stubborn, base, and wicked." Then Lee crowned his diatribe with an astonishingly casual remark which to the modern reader comes as a perverse anti-climax: "Whether this proceeds from a native baseness that fits their minds for all villany; or that they never receive the benefit of education, I shall not presume to determine." Fifty years earlier, Lee would have felt no need to express his hesitation: rather, he would have seen nothing to hesitate about. In 1764 however, he could roundly denounce the Negro and then calmly declare that he was uncertain whether the Negro's baseness was innate. He sensed the question which has since become so clear—and saw no pressing need to answer it.

On this fundamental question of nature versus nurture, as well as on so many related questions concerning the

Negro, the Revolutionary era marked a critical turning point. From the Revolution on, the increasingly acrimonious debates on the Negro's nature were grounded in assumptions which, in contrast to those prevailing in pre-Revolutionary America, have a decidely modern timbre. During this third quarter of the eighteenth century, many Americans awoke to the fact that a hitherto unquestioned social institution had spread its roots not only throughout the economic structure of much of the country but into their own minds. As they became conscious of this infiltration they came to recognize that enslavement of the Negro depended upon their assessment of him, that Negro slavery existed within themselves, within their "prejudices," particularly "in Relation to Colour." For equalitarians of whatever stripe, there were two possible ways of effecting a change in the white man's mind. Both necessarily involved an end to slavery, since slavery impaired the feeling of brotherhood within the white man and still more obviously presented an obstacle to the Negro's becoming the white man's equal in actuality. Appeal to environment provided an answer on both counts, and Americans plumped eagerly for a mode of thinking which afforded a prospect of dramatic change both in the Negro and within themselves.

This heightened self-consciousness with which environmentalist thinking was so closely connected was itself closely linked to the crisis known as the American Revolution. Indeed in an important sense the Revolution *was* a great awakening of English colonials in America. The radical change in Americans' thinking about the mother country was equally a change in thinking about themselves. The rise of antislavery sentiment also represented a process of self-evaluation, an integral part of what John Adams recalled as "this radical change in the principles, opinions, sentiments, and affections of the people." The "real American Revolution" involved a newly intense scrutiny of colonial society including the peculiarly un-English institution of Negro slavery.

American thinking about the status of Negroes could never again be characterized by placid and unheeding acceptance. As a standing contradiction of age-old presuppositions about the equality of men, slavery cried out for a revival of public morality. As an inward sin, slavery invited the reform without which Americans could never expect success as an independent people. As a violation of the ideology of equal rights, slavery mocked the ideals upon which the new republic was founded.

The American Revolution: CONGRESS, JULY 4, 1776

...of the thirteen united States of America...

Whose Revolution?

# The Role and Status of Women

JOHN TODD WHITE (b. 1944) examines the role of some Revolutionary women in the War for American Independence, specifically the group known as "camp followers." Some were in the pay of the armies, others traveled along just to be with their husbands or lovers. In a few cases, they were prostitutes or even rum-runners. George Washington disliked having women in his army, but because of manpower shortages he could not afford to lose the men who might be offended if their wives or consorts were not permitted in camp. As White demonstrates, the camp followers have been treated with sugar-coated gentility by most historians and archivists, when actually the reality was something quite different. White suggests that the distinctions made between presumed male and female roles that can be found in the records of the middle and upper classes were not valid for the lower orders, especially in the military environment. Was this a small, though admittedly unusual, beginning for women's rights, or was it a peculiarity of the times that left no permanent imprint?

# The Truth About Molly Pitcher

On June 28, 1778, the American Revolutionary Army engaged the British forces at Monmouth Court House, New Jersey, During the pitched battle that followed, an anonymous woman was observed taking part in the combat. Despite the fact that there are only two known contemporary accounts of a woman soldier at the Battle of Monmouth, a pleasant, but misleading, legend has developed around the woman known today as "Molly Pitcher."

The documentary basis for the Molly Pitcher legend is both limited and contradictory. Dr. Albigence Waldo, a military surgeon, recorded the event in his diary a few days after it happened, but he did not witness it himself and only reported what he had been told by a wounded officer. In Waldo's account the woman's husband was killed, and though the doctor was imprecise in his use of terms, it appears that the weapon the woman took up was her husband's musket. The other piece of documentary evidence is contained in the memoir of a soldier written fifty-two years later. Joseph Plumb Martin, unlike Albigence Waldo, actually witnessed the event. His account states that the woman's husband was in the artillery and that she served beside him "the whole time."

Legends rarely develop from documentary evidence and the story of Molly Pitcher is no exception. Indeed, the contemporary accounts only came to light once people began to search for evidence with which to confirm or deny written history which was based on oral tradition. One strand of this oral tradition, for example, has centered on the personage of Mary McCauly of Carlisle, Pennsylvania. Residents of Carlisle remembered, long after "Molly" McCauly's death, that she claimed to have taken some part in the Battle of Monmouth. These remembrances, though varied, form a large part of the legend of Molly Pitcher. Other strands of oral tradition which maintain the anonymity of the woman gunner at Monmouth have been even more varied in content. Considering the lack of documentary evidence and the fact that much of the legend is based on oral tradition, it is not surprising that the "truth" about Molly Pitcher is, at best, confusing. Molly has been identified as both Irish and German. Her age has differed by as much as a decade. Her actions at the Battle of Monmouth include carrying water to thirsty troops, or firing a cannon, or both. Accounts that maintain she carried water cannot agree on whether she used a pitcher, a bucket, or a canteen, nor is there any consensus on whether

the water was for her husband at the cannon or for the infantrymen in the field. Her husband is said to have served in the infantry, the artillery, or both. Many accounts claim that he was killed during the battle, some suggest that he was only wounded, and one of the two eyewitness accounts states that Molly served by her husband's side the entire time. The alleged rewards for Molly's herosim include half-pay, a pension, a single gold piece, or an official commission as sergeant or lieutenant. She has been known by various names including Captain Molly, Molly Maban, Molly Hanna, Moll Pitcher, Molly Pitcher, Mary Ludwig Hays McCauly and, most recently, Mary Hays McCauly without the maiden name of Ludwig.

One of the most interesting things about the Molly Pitcher legend is the fact that that pseudonym is of relatively recent origin, first appearing in print on the eve of the Civil War. Where the anonymous woman gunner of Monmouth is given a name in earlier accounts it is not Molly Pitcher but Captain Molly. Were Captain Molly and Molly Pitcher the same person? Benson J. Lossing, an early student of the American Revolution, claimed they were not. "Art and romance," he argued, had confused two different women; Captain Molly was actually the heroine of Monmouth.

Lossing's account of Captain Molly states that after the war she was known as a hard-drinking woman who reportedly died of syphillis in a state of poverty. Much of Lossing's account of Captain Molly corresponds to that of a positively identifiable camp follower-turned-artillery assistant by the name of Margaret Corbin. Margaret

Corbin not only fits Lossing's picture of a broken and destitute woman, but, also, much of the Molly Pitcher Legend. Like Molly, Margaret's husband was in the artillery. When he was killed at the battle for Fort Washington in November 1776 she took his position at the cannon. She was seriously wounded during the fighting and, as a result, was pensioned by the Continental Congress.

Margaret Corbin has gained little historical recognition for her courageous act. At the same time that the unidentified woman at the Battle of Monmouth who was subsequently dubbed Molly Pitcher was becoming an enduring heroine, Margaret Corbin was fading into historical obscurity. It is not difficult to understand why. Margaret Corbin, like her sister camp followers, was not the stuff of which the nineteenth century made heroines. "Dirty Kate," a name by which Lossing reported she was known, simply could not be put forth as an object of honor and emulation.

It is, however, as a camp follower of the American Revolution that Molly Pitcher derives her true significance rather than as a daring female who appeared on the battlefield as if from nowhere and transcended the limitations of her sex. The "truth" about Molly Pitcher is the story of the women who followed their husbands during the Revolutionary War.

Many of these women are anonymous and will probably remain so. The vast records generated by the military conflict have, however, preserved sufficient data on which to base some tentative conclusions about them. The pension application file of Margaret Shortridge who was with her husband at Fort Washington near Portsmouth, New Hampshire, contains a description of her that may be extended to all camp followers: "She is poor, and she always has been. . . . She always said her husband realized but very little for all he ever received from the Government for his services—I have no doubt of this fact from her always having been poor."

Margaret Shortridge was more fortunate than many camp followers. Rather than moving with the army through the countryside, she served in her home region. She and her husband had grown up near where he was stationed but, even so, she moved as close to the fort as possible. It was in a house outside Fort Washington that she bore her first child in the winter of 1778–1779. Her husband John stated that he was a farmer when he enlisted in Captain Titus Salter's artillery company. It is doubtful, however, that he owned much if any property, for when his enlistment expired, he and Margaret moved to a different section of New Hampshire.

John Shortridge, like his wife, was illiterate, always signing documents with his mark. His only source of income was his military pay. With his fellow soldiers, he periodically demanded that the New Hampshire legislature increase his wages. In one case, the artillery company requested a share of the prize money from a captured vessel so that they might have something with which to sustain their families in those times of "General Distress." In another petition, the same men contended that their wages were not sufficient to support their families. They informed the legislature that they did not wish to get rich;

" . . . we only Beg wages to Live By. . . . "

Rebecca Morgan Leggett was another camp follower. Unlike Margaret Shortridge, Rebecca was a refugee who left Long Island under a flag of truce and married her husband Abraham shortly thereafter. Her case is also somewhat unusual because her husband was a junior officer. Evidence indicates that the lower-ranking officers generally left wives at home. The correspondence of Joseph and Sarah Hodgkins, for example, shows that, despite loneliness and difficulty, it was preferable for a woman to remain with the family property and in the vicinity of friends and relatives rather than enduring the hardships of army life. Why, then, did Rebecca Leggett accompany her husband? While officers were normally selected from the middle and upper classes, Abraham Leggett was one of those men thrust into a position of authority and responsibility by the Revolution. His decision to take his wife to camp reflected his social origins rather than his newly-found status as a Continental officer.

Leggett's father had died of the fever while on a military expedition during the Seven Years War. The boy was seven years old at the time. Living first with a grandfather and then an uncle, Abraham was apprenticed to a blacksmith at the age of fourteen. The smith, however, abused the trust and used the boy for farm labor instead of teaching him the trade. Three years later Leggett was apprenticed to another blacksmith, but by 1775 there was little business and he went to work in the Continental shipyards. Shortly thereafter he enlisted on the American side, unexpectedly receiving a com-mission as a lieutenant in the beginning of 1777. Clearly, Leggett's background was much the same as that of many of the common soldiers from whose ranks he was lifted by fortune and, like them, he took his wife to camp. Fortunately, Rebecca, who was pregnant by October when her husband was captured, had somewhere else to go rather than follow him into captivity.

Unlike Margaret Shortridge and Rebecca Leggett, Nancy Adams met her husband after he was already in the army. She lived in Virginia and met Francis Adams, a trumpeter in Colonel William Washington's cavalry, when the army moved into her state in preparation for the final offensive against Cornwallis. Possibly Nancy and Francis had a common law marriage. Certainly there was no elaborate ceremony, at best a few words spoken by a chaplain or an officer. Still, it was an unusually stable union, for they remained together for over fifty years, until Francis died. When Nancy filed for a widow's pension she could not remember the day, month or year in which she was married, only that it had taken place sometime before the capture of Cornwallis. She had no certificate, nor could she produce or even name any witnesses to the marriage ceremony. She could only adduce on her behalf a daughter and an acquaintance. Her daughter, Susannah Cummins, testified that her mother and father " . . . lived together as man and wife, and no question has ever been made as to the legality of their marriage." Robert McAfee, a friend of the family, testified that Francis and Nancy Adams " . . . lived together & was reputed as Man & Wife. . . . The said

Adams often told me that he was married while in the Army about the time or shortly after the surrender of Lord Cornwallis's army. . . . They have passed as man and wife and so lived together. . . . "

Forced from their homes by the British, following their husbands or marrying soldiers they met, women joined the army. Once there, though officially tolerated, they were often an embarrassment and an annoyance to the commander in chief. When the army passed through Philadelphia on its way to confront General William Howe in 1777, Washington issued express orders that "Not a woman belonging to the army is to be seen with the troops on their march thro' the city." Frequently, but with little effect, Washington tried to reduce the number of women. "In the present marching state of the army, every incumberance proves greatly prejudical to the service; the multitude of women in particular, especially those who are pregnant, or have children are a clog upon every movement." He directed his subordinate officers to use "every reasonable method in their power to get rid of all such as are not absolutely necessary. . . . "

If we can sympathize with Washington, however, it is difficult to understand why historians have exhibited a similar degree of annoyance and embarrassment toward the camp followers. Indeed, most historians seem to believe that following the army was desirable. Quite the reverse was true. Life in the army was severe. To assume that women would voluntarily accept the hardships of camp life if there had been any alternative is absurd. Nevertheless, these women are always portrayed as serving the troops in traditional female roles almost as though they needed to earn the dubious luxury of following the army. In the words of Walter Hart Blumenthal, the author of the only book on female camp followers, the women who "went along with the patriot army, washed, mended and cooked for the men." Whether in the farmhouse or on the battlefield, it seems that woman's place must have been in the home.

There is, however, very little documentary evidence to support this view of battlefield domesticity, and a good deal which argues against it. In fact, the evidence suggests that the distinctions between male and female roles which are to be found in the records of the middle and upper classes were lacking in the lower socio-economic strata, particularly in the military environment. The records left by common soldiers of the Revolution clearly indicate that they, not the women camp followers were doing their own cooking, sewing, and washing. Take, for example, the journal entries of Nahum Parker, age seventeen: June 19, "I got my Trouses Cut out"; June 12, "I got my Trowses made to Day"; June 25, "I mended my Shoes"; August 21, "I got my Shirt washt." These domestic chores did not seem to bother young Parker, for in the midst of them he wrote "A Lazzy Mery Life who would not be A Soldier."

If Nahum Parker was doing his own drudge work and not seeming to mind, what were the women doing? They, of course, did their own washing, sewing, and cooking, but for the most part they were merely trying to survive under adverse circumstances. After the Battle of Bemis Heights, for example, it was reported that the American camp women stripped the British dead of their clothing. In addition to stripping the dead, the women plundered captured flour and stole from other Americans. In December 1779, one Mrs. Thomas was drummed out of Israel Angell's Second Rhode Island Regiment for stealing a dress. Perhaps her guilt was established by the possession of a gown that was described as "very handsom." Interestingly, except for not being whipped, her treatment was little different than that accorded male soldiers: "I . . . ordered all the Drums and fifes to parade and Drum her out of the Regt. with a paper pind to her back with these words in Cappital letters, /A THIEF/ thus She off with Musick—"

The camp follower was an unpolished woman. She did not even approach the eighteenth-century definition of a lady. She followed the army while pregnant and gave birth to her children in the squalor of military hospitals or on baggage wagons. She stole, swore, drank, and, when the occasion arose, she could fight as well. An important part of the Molly Pitcher legend has been the assumption that a single "Molly" stood alone in her direct contribution to the military effort. In fact, we know that Mary Hays McCauly was not the only woman cannoneer. Margaret Corbin preceded her in the category nineteen months earlier. Not only did Margaret fire a cannon, but she was seriously wounded. There is also a story, generally attached to either Molly Pitcher or Margaret Corbin, of a woman firing a cannon at Fort Clinton in October 1777. Yet neither Mary Hays McCauly nor Margaret Corbin was present at Fort

Clinton, so if the story is true, there was at least one more woman gunner.

It is possible to speculate that women were more regularly involved in combat than has been suspected. While tactical and technological factors served to separate women from the infantry, such was not the case with the artillery. During the eighteenth century, artillery was, for all practical purposes, stationary once it was deployed. Normally it was removed from the direct force of the battle as a result of its placement on the flanks or at the rear of the field. Furthermore, it was rarely the object of attack. Rather, both sides employed their artillery against the opposing infantry upon which it could do the most damage. Because the artillery was immobile and removed from direct fire, access to it was relatively easy for the women camp followers.

If access was provided, there was also a reason for the presence of women at the front. Water was an essential element in the firing artillery, for after the cannon was discharged, the barrel had to be swabbed with water prior to reloading to prevent the premature ignition of the new charge. Writers have usually assumed that "Molly" was carrying drinking water to thirsty soldiers, when in fact she was probably engaged in a more essential military task. It is clearly possible, even likely, that undermanned artillery units would regularly employ women camp followers, wives of the gunners, in bringing water to the cannon. Once a woman was on the scene, the transition from water bearer to cannoneer was not particularly difficult. Firing a cannon was not a one-man operation; at the very least, three were required. If a member of a gun crew were disabled, the efficiency of the weapon would be seriously impaired. A woman who was present might easily complete the number of persons necessary to operate the cannon, especially if she had previously observed the cannoneers carrying out their assignments.

This speculation is supported by contemporary evidence. Joseph Plumb Martin, the only eyewitness to record seeing a woman fighting in the battle of Monmouth, wrote:

One little incident happened during the heat of the cannonade, which I was eyewitness to, and which I think would be unpardonable not to mention. A woman whose husband belonged to the artillery and who was then attached to a piece in the engagement, attended with her husband at the piece the whole time. While in the act of reaching a cartridge and having one of her feet as far before the other as she could step, a cannon shot from the enemy passed directly between her legs without doing any other damage then carrying away all the lower part of her petticoat. Looking at it with apparent unconcern, she observed that it was lucky it did not pass a little higher, for in that case it might have carried away something else, and continued her occupation.

It should be noted that the source of this quote, a soldier who served throughout the war, seems to have taken the woman's presence for granted. The emphasis is not on the presence of the woman but on the fact that something unusual happened to her. She "attended with her husband at the piece the whole time," and after the incident she "continued her occupa-tion." There is no mention of spartan feminism or everlasting glory, merely the fact that she was there and then the anecdote. In the final analysis, the assumption that Molly Pitcher was an aberration is not supported by the evidence.

The Molly Pitcher legend which developed in the nineteenth century transformed an unknown camp follower into an acceptable picture of middle class femininity. The preservation of the woman's anonymity during the development of an oral tradition allowed her to be converted from a rugged, unpolished member of the lower classes into a pretty young women whose presence on the battlefield was explained by the fact that she was tending to the needs of men. By the time a woman was put forth as the true Molly Pitcher no one was willing to challenge what one nineteenth century writer referred to as the "romance" of a story which was "dear and *true to the national heart.*"

The Molly Pitcher legend is doubly unfortunate. The oral tradition that grew up around the anonymous woman at Monmouth allowed people to forget the real contributions of Margaret Corbin. But, if Molly Pitcher was more acceptable than Margaret Corbin, at least she remained a camp follower. Once a name was attached to the legend even this fact was deemphasized. The story of Molly Pitcher not only denied the personal achievements of one woman, it also obscured the contributions of the female members of an entire social class to the winning of American independence.

MARY BETH NORTON (b. 1943) has done extensive
work on loyalists of the American Revolutionary era,
including her study *The British-Americans: The Loyalist Exiles in England, 1774–1789.* Her essay focuses
on loyalist women, who were often verbally abused,
imprisoned, and threatened with bodily harm even
when they had not taken an active part in opposing
the insurgents. Evidence drawn from the Loyalists'
Claims Commission, which was established in England
after the War for Independence to compensate
"tories" for losses sustained during the war, also
strongly suggests, according to Norton, that the lives
of most late eighteenth-century women revolved
around their households, either by choice or by the
force of social convention. Indeed, the role and
sphere of all American women may have become
more rigidly defined within the context of the concept of "republican motherhood." Why did women,
whether camp followers or loyalists, seem to gain so
little from the Revolution and its ideology of liberty?
Did the fault lie in the nature of the Revolution, or
were other factors more important?

# Revolutionary Women in Peace and War: The Case of the Loyalists

In recent years historians have come
to recognize the central role of the
family in the shaping of American
society. Especially in the eighteenth
century, when "household" and "family" were synonymous terms, and when
household manufactures constituted a
major contribution to the economy,
the person who ran the household—
the wife and mother—occupied a posi-

From Mary Beth Norton, "Eighteenth-Century American Women in Peace and War:
The Case of the Loyalists," *William and Mary Quarterly,* 3rd Sers., XXXIII (1976), pp. 386–
409. Reprinted by permission of the Institute of Early American History and Culture and
the author. Footnotes omitted.

tion of crucial significance. Yet those who have studied eighteenth-century women have usually chosen to focus on a few outstanding, perhaps unrepresentative individuals, such as Eliza Lucas Pinckney, Abigail Smith Adams, and Mercy Otis Warren. They have also emphasized the activities of women outside the home and have concentrated on the prescriptive literature of the day. Little has been done to examine in depth the lives actually led by the majority of colonial women or to assess the impact of the Revolution upon them.

Such a study can illuminate a number of important topics. Demographic scholars are beginning to discover the dimensions of eighteenth-century households, but a knowledge of size alone means little without a delineation of roles filled by husband and wife within those households. Historians of nineteenth-century American women have analyzed the ideology which has been termed the "cult of true womanhood" or the "cult of domesticity," but the relationship of these ideas to the lives of women in the preceding century remains largely unexplored. And although some historians of the Revolution now view the war as a socially disruptive phenomenon, they have not yet applied that insight specifically to the study of the family.

Fortunately, at least one set of documents contains material relevant to an investigation of all these aspects of late eighteenth-century American family life: the 281 volumes of the loyalist claims, housed at the Public Record Office in London. Although these manuscripts have been used extensively for political and economic studies

of loyalism, they have only once before been utilized for an examination of colonial society. What makes the loyalist claims uniquely useful is the fact that they contain information not only about the personal wartime experiences of thousands of Americans but also about the modes of life the war disrupted.

Among the 3,225 loyalists who presented claims to the British government after the war were 468 American refugee women. The analysis that follows is based upon an examination of the documents—formal memorials, loss schedules, and private letters—submitted by these women to the loyalist claims commission, and on the commission's nearly verbatim records of the women's personal appearances before them. These women cannot be said to compose a statistically reliable sample of American womanhood. It is entirely possible that loyalist families differed demographically and economically, as well as politically, from their revolutionary neighbors, and it is highly probable that the refugee claimants did not accurately represent even the loyalist population, much less that of colonies as a whole. Nonetheless, the 468 claimants included white women of all descriptions, from every colony and all social and economic levels: they were educated and illiterate; married, widowed, single, and deserted; rural and urban; wealthy, middling, and poverty-stricken. Accordingly, used with care, the loyalist claims can tell us much about the varieties of female experience in America in the third quarter of the eighteenth century.

One aspect of prewar family life that is systematically revealed in the claims documents is the economic relationship of husband and wife within the household. All claimants, male and female alike, had to supply the commission with detailed estimates of property losses. Given the circumstances of war, documentary evidence such as deeds, bills of sale, and wills was rarely available in complete form, and the commission therefore relied extensively upon the sworn testimony of the claimants and their witnesses in assessing losses. The claimants had nothing to gain by withholding information, because the amount of compensation they received depended in large part on their ability to describe their losses. Consequently, it may be assumed that what the loyalists told the commission, both orally and in writing, represented the full extent of their knowledge of their families' income and property. The women's claims thus make it possible to determine the nature of their participation in the financial affairs of their households.

Strikingly, although male loyalists consistently supplied detailed assessments of the worth of their holdings, many women were unable to place precise valuations on the property for which they claimed compensation. Time after time similar phrases appear in the records of oral testimony before the commission: "She cant say what the Houses cost or what they would have sold for" (the widow of a Norfolk merchant); "Says she is much a Stranger to the state of Her Husband's Concerns" (the widow of a storekeeper from Ninety-Six, South Carolina); "It was meadow Land, she cannot speak of the Value" (a New Jersey farmer's widow); "Her husband was a Trader and had many Debts owing to him She does not know how much they

amounted to" (a widow from Ninety-Six); "She can't speak to the Value of the Stock in Trade" (a Rhode Island merchant's widow); "It was a good Tract but does not know how to value it" (the widow of a Crown Point farmer).

Even when women submitted detailed loss schedules in writing, they frequently revealed at their oral examinations that they had relied on male relatives or friends, or even on vaguely recalled statements made by their dead husbands, in arriving at the apparently knowledgeable estimates they had initially given to the commission. For example, a New Jersey woman, questioned about her husband's annual income, referred the commissioners to her father and other male witnesses, admitting that she did not know the amount he had earned. Similarly, the widow of a Charleston saddler told the commissioners that "she does not know the Amount of Her husband's Property, but she remembers to have heard him say in the year 1777 that he was worth £2,000 sterling clear of all Debts." Such statements abound in the claims records: "She is unable to speak to the value of the Plantn herself, but refers to Mr. Cassills"; "Says she cannot speak to the Value—the Valuatn was made by Capt McDonald and Major Munro"; Says her Son in Law Capt Douglas is better acquainted with the particulars of her property than herself and she refers to him for an Account thereof."

Although many female claimants thus lacked specific knowledge of their families' finances, there were substantial variations within the general pattern. The very wealthiest women—like Isabella Logan of Virginia (who could say only that she and her husband had lived in "a new Elegant, large double Brick House with two wings all finish'd in the best taste with articles from London") and Mrs. Egerton Leigh of South Carolina (who gave it as her opinion that her husband had "a considerable real Estate as well as personal property . . . worth more than £10,000 . . . tho' she cannot herself speak to it with accuracy")—also tended to be the ones most incapable of describing their husband's business affairs. Yet some wealthy, well-educated women were conversant with nearly every detail of the family finances. For the most part, this latter group was composed of women who had brought the property they described to their husbands at marriage or who had been widowed before the war and had served as executrixes of the estates in question for some time. A case in point is that of Sarah Gould Troutbeck, daughter, executrix, and primary heir of John Gould, a prosperous Boston merchant. Her husband John, an Anglican clergyman, died in 1778, and so she carried the full burden of presenting the family's claim to the commission. Although she deprecatingly described herself to the board as "a poor weak Woman unused to business," she supplied the commissioners with detailed evidence of her losses and unrelentingly pursued her debtors. "Your not hearing from me for so long a time may induce you to think I have relinquished my claim to the interest due on your note," she informed one man in 1788. "If you realy entertain any such thoughts I must beg leave to undeceive you." In addition, she did what few loyalists of either sex had the courage to at-tempt—return to the United States to try to recover her property. When she arrived in 1785, she found her estates "in the greatest confusion" but nevertheless managed within several months to repossess one house and to collect some debts. In the end she apparently won restoration of most of her holdings.

Yet not all the female loyalists who had inherited property in their own right were as familiar with it as was Sarah Troutbeck. Another Massachusetts woman admitted to the commissioners that she did not know the value of the 550 acres left her by a relative, or even how much of the land was cultivated. "Her Brother managed everything for her and gave her what Money she wanted," she explained. In the same vein, a New Yorker was aware that her father had left her some property in his will, but "she does not know what property." A Charleston resident who had owned a house jointly with her brother commented that "it was a good House," but the commission noted, "she does not know the Value of it." And twice-widowed Jane Gibbes, claiming for the farms owned by her back-country South Carolina husbands, told the commission that she had relied on neighbors to assess the worth of the property, for "she can't speak positively to the value of her Lands herself."

But if Jane Gibbs could not precisely evaluate the farms she had lived on, she still knew a good deal about them. She described the total acreage, the amount of land under cultivation, the crops planted, and the livestock that had been lost. In this she was representative of most rural female loyalists with claims that were not complicated by the existence of mortgages or outstanding debts. Although they did not always know the exact value of the land for which they requested reimbursement, they could supply the commission with many important details about the family property: the number of cattle, horses, sheep, and hogs; the types of tools used; the acreage planted, and with what crops; the amounts of grain and other foodstuffs stored for the winter; and the value of such unusual possessions as beehives or a "Covering Horse." It was when they were asked about property on which they had not lived, about debts owed by their husbands, or about details of wills or mortgages that they most often admitted ignorance.

A good example is Mary McAlpin, who had settled with her husband on a farm near Saratoga, New York, in 1767. She did not know what her husband had paid for some unimproved lands, or the acreage of another farm he had purchased, but she was well acquainted with the property on which they had lived. The farm, she told the commissioners, "had been wholly cleared and Improved and was in the most perfect State of Cultivation." There were two "Log Houses plaistered and floored," one for them and one for their hired laborers, and sufficient materials on hand to build "a large and Commodious Brick House." Her husband had planted wheat, rye, peas, oats, barley, corn, turnips, potatoes, and melons; and "the Meadows had been laid down or sown with Clover and Timothy Grass, the two kind of Grass Seeds most Valued in that Country." The McAlpins had had a kitchen garden that produced "in great abundance every Vegi-

table usually cultivated in that part of America." Moreover, the farm was "well Provided" with such utensils as "a Team waggon, Carts sledges Carwls [sic] Wheels for Waggons, Wheels for Carts, Wheelbarrows, drags for Timber Ploughs, Harrows Hay Sythes Brush Sythes Grubbling Harrows, and all sorts of Carpenters Tools Shoemakers Tools Shovels, Spades, Axes Iron Crow Barrs etc."

After offering all these details, however, Mrs. McAlpin proved unable to assess the value of the property accurately. She gave the commission a total claim of £6,000, clearly an estimate, and when asked to break down a particular item on her schedule into its component parts she could not do so, saying that "She valued the Whole in the Lump in that Sum." Moreover, she proved ignorant of the terms of her husband's will, confusedly telling the commissioners that he had "left his real personal Estate to his Son—This she supposes was his Lands" (the board's secretary noted carefully, "This is her own Expression"), when in fact she had been left a life interest in the real estate plus half the personal estate. In short, Mary McAlpin typifies the rural female claimant, though her husband's property was substantially larger than average. She knew what he had owned, but she did not know exactly how much it was worth. She was well acquainted with the day-to-day operations of the farm but understood very little about the general family finances. And she knew nothing at all about legal or business terminology.

The pattern for urban dwellers was more varied. In the first place, included in their number were most of the wealthy women mentioned earlier, both those who knew little or nothing about their husbands' estates and those who, like Sarah Troutbeck, were conversant with the family holdings. Secondly, a higher percentage of urban women engaged directly in business. Among the 468 female claimants there were forty-three who declared either that they had earned money on their own or that they had assisted their husbands in some way. Only three of these forty-three can be described as rural: a tavern keeper's wife from Ticonderoga, a small shopkeeper from Niagara, and the housekeeper for the family of Col. Guy Johnson. All the other working women came from cities such as Boston, Philadelphia, Charleston, and New York, or from smaller but substantial towns like Williamsburg, Wilmington, N.C., and Baltimore. The urban women's occupations were as varied as the urban centers in which they resided. There were ten who took lodgers, eighteen shopkeepers and merchants of various sorts, five tavern-keepers, four milliners, two mantua makers, a seamstress, a midwife, an owner of a coffeehouse, a schoolteacher, a printer, one who did not specify an occupation, and two prostitutes who described themselves as owners of a small shop and declared that their house had been "always open" to British officers needing "aid and attention."

As might be expected, the women who had managed businesses or assisted their husbands (one wrote that she was "truly his Partner" in a "steady Course of painfull Industry") were best informed about the value of their property. Those who had been grocers or milliners could usually list in detail the stock they had lost; the midwife had witnesses to support her claim to a high annual income from her profession; the boardinghouse keepers knew what they had spent for furniture and supplies; and the printer could readily value her shop's equipment. But even those working women could not give a full report on all aspects of their husbands' holdings: the widow of a Boston storekeeper, for example, could accurately list their stock in trade but admitted ignorance of the value of the property her husband had inherited from his father, and although the widow of another Boston merchant had carried on the business after her husband was wounded at Bunker Hill, she was not familiar with the overall value of their property.

It is therefore not surprising that women claimants on the average received a smaller return on their claims than did their male counterparts. Since the Commissioners reimbursed only for fully proven losses, the amounts awarded are a crude indicator of the relative ability of individual refugees to describe their losses and to muster written and oral evidence on their own behalf. If women had known as much as their husbands about the family estates, there would have been little or no difference between the average amounts granted to each sex. But of the claims heard in England for which complete information is available, 660 loyalist men received an average return of 39.5 percent, while for 71 women the figure was 34.1 percent. And this calculation does not take into account the large number of women's claims, including some submitted by businesswomen, which were entirely disallowed for lack of proof.

In the absence of data for other time periods and populations, it is difficult to assess the significance of the figures that show that slightly less than 10 percent (9.2 percent, to be exact) of the loyalist refugee women worked outside the home. Historians have tended to stress the widespread participation of colonial women in economic enterprise, usually as a means of distinguishing them from their reputedly more confined nineteenth-century counterparts. The claims documents demonstrate that some women engaged in business, either alone or with their husbands, but 9.2 percent may be either a large or a small proportion of the total female population, depending on how one looks at it. The figures themselves must remain somewhat ambiguous, at least until additional data are obtained. What is not at all ambiguous, however, is the distinctive pattern of the female claimant's knowledge.

For regardless of whether they came from rural or urban areas, and regardless of their background or degree of participation in business, the loyalist women testified almost exclusively on the basis of their knowledge of those parts of the family property with which their own lives brought them into regular contact. What they uniformly lacked were those pieces of information about business matters that could have been supplied only by their husbands. Evidently, late eighteenth-century American men, at least those who became loyalists, did not systematically discuss matters of family finances with their wives. From that fact it may be inferred that the men—and their wives as well, perhaps—accepted the dictum that woman's

place was in the home. After all, that was where more than 90 percent of the loyalist women stayed, and their ignorance of the broader aspects of their families' economic circumstances indicates that their interest in such affairs was either minimal or else deliberately thwarted by their husbands.

It would therefore appear that the 9 percent figure for working women is evidence not of a climate favorable to feminine enterprise but rather of the opposite: women were expected to remain largely within the home unless forced by necessity, such as the illness or death of their husbands, to do otherwise. The fact that fewer than one-half (seventeen, to be precise) of the working women enumerated earlier had healthy, living husbands at the time they engaged in business leads toward the same conclusion. The implication is that in mid-eighteenth-century America woman's sphere was rigidly defined at all levels of society, not merely in the wealthy households in which this phenomenon has been recognized.

This tentative conclusion is supported by evidence drawn from another aspect of the claims, for a concomitant of the contention that colonial women often engaged in business endeavors has been the assertion that colonial men, as the theoretical and legal heads of household, frequently assumed a large share of domestic responsibilities. Yet if men had been deeply involved in running their households—in keeping accounts and making purchases, even if not in doing day-to-day chores—they should have described household furnishings in much the same detail as their wives used. But just as female claimants were unable to delineate their husbands' business dealings accurately, so men separated from their wives—regardless of their social status—failed to submit specific lists of lost household items like furniture, dishes, or kitchen utensils. One such refugee observed to the commission in 1788, "As Household Furniture consists of a Variety of Articles, at this distance of time I cannot sufficiently recollect them so as to fix a Value on them to the Satisfaction of my mind." It is impossible to imagine a loyalist woman making a comparable statement. For her, what to a man was simply "a Variety of Articles" resolved itself into such familiar and cherished objects as "1 Compleat set blue and white Tea and Table China," "a Large new Goose feather Bed, bolster Pillows and Bedstead," "a Small painted Book Case and Desk," "1 Japan Tea Board," "2 smoothing Irons," and "1 old brass Coffee Pott." Moreover, although men usually noted losses of clothing in a general way, by listing a single undifferentiated sum, women frequently claimed for specific articles of jewelry and apparel. For example, Mary Swords of Saratoga disclosed that she had lost to rebel plunderers a "Long Scarlet Cloak" and a "Velvet Muff and Tippett," in addition to "One pair of Ear Rings French paste set in Gold," "One small pair of Ear Rings Garnets," and "one Gold Broatch with a small diamond Top."

The significance of such lists lies not only in the fact that they indicate what kinds of property the claimants knew well enough to describe accurately and in detail, but also in the insight they provide into the possessions which claimants thought were sufficiently important to mention individually. For example, a rural New York woman left no doubt about her pride in "a fine large new stove"; a resident of Manhattan carefully noted that one of her lost beds was covered in "Red Damask"; and a Rhode Islander called attention to the closets in her "large new dwelling house." The differentiated contents of men's and women's claims thus take on more importance, since the contrasting lists not only suggest the extent of the claimants' knowledge but also reveal their assessments of the relative importance of their possessions. To men, furniture, dishes, and clothing could easily be lumped together under general headings; to women, such possessions had to be carefully enumerated and described.

In the end, all of the evidence that can be drawn from the loyalist claims points to the conclusion that the lives of the vast majority of women in the Revolutionary era revolved around their immediate households to a notable degree. The economic function of those households in relation to the family property largely determined the extent of their knowledge of that property. In rural areas, where women's household chores included caring for the stock and perhaps occasionally working in the fields, women were conversant with a greater proportion of the family estates than were urban women, whose knowledge was for the most part confined to the furnishings of the houses in which they lived, unless they had been widowed before the war or had worked outside the home. The wealth of the family was thus a less significant determinant of the woman's role than was the nature of the household. To be sure, at the extreme ends of the economic scale, wealth and education, or the lack of them, affected a woman's comprehension of her family's property, but what the women displayed were relative degrees of ignorance. If the loyalist claimants are at all representative, very few married colonial women were familiar with the broader aspects of their families' financial affairs. Regardless of where they lived, they were largely insulated from the agricultural and business worlds in which their husbands engaged daily. As a result, the Revolutionary War, which deprived female loyalists of the households in which they had lived and worked, and which at the same time forced them to confront directly the wider worlds of which they had had little previous knowledge, was for them an undeniably traumatic experience.

At the outbreak of the war, loyalist women expected that "their Sex and the Humanity of a civilized People" would protect them from "disrespectfull Indignities." Most of them soon learned otherwise. Rebel men may have paid lip service to the ideal that women and children should be treated as noncombatants but in practice they consigned female loyalists to much the same fate as their male relatives. Left behind by their fleeing husbands (either because of the anticipated difficulties of a journey to the British lines or in the hope that the family property might thereby be preserved), loyalist wives, with their children, frequently found themselves "stripped of every Thing" by American troops who, as one woman put it, "not contented with possessing themselves of her property were disposed to visit severity upon her person and

Those of her friends." Female loyalists were often verbally abused, imprisoned, and threatened with bodily harm even when they had not taken an active role in opposing the rebel cause.

When they had assisted the British—and many aided prisoners or gathered intelligence—their fate was far worse. For example, the New Yorker Lorenda Holmes, who carried letters through the lines in 1776, was stripped by an angry band of committeemen and dragged "to the Drawing Room Window . . . exposing her to many Thousands of People Naked." On this occasion Mrs. Holmes admitted that she "recieved no wounds or bruises from them only shame and horror of the Mind," but a few months later, after she had shown some refugees the way to the British camp, an American officer came to her house and held her "right foot upon the Coals until he had burnt it in a most shocking manner," telling her "he would learn her to carry off Loyalists to the British Army."

As can readily be imagined, the women did not come through such experiences emotionally unscathed. One Massachusetts mother reported that her twelve-year-old daughter suffered from "nervous Fits" as a result of "the usage she met with from the Mobs"; and another New England woman, the wife of a merchant who was an early target of the local committee because he resisted the non-importation movement, described to a female friend her reaction to a threatening letter they had received: "I have never injoyed one hours real Sattisfaction since the receipt of that Dreadfull Letter my mind is in continual agitation and the very rustling of the

Trees alarms me." Some time later the same woman was unfortunate enough to be abused by a rebel militiaman. After that incident, she reported, "I did not recover from my fright for several days. The sound of drum or the sight of a gun put me into such a tremor that I could not command myself." It was only natural for these women to look forward with longing to the day when they could escape to Canada or, better still, to England, "a land of peace, liberty and plenty." It seemed to them that their troubles would end when they finally left America. But, as one wrote later with the benefit of hindsight, their "severest trials were just begun."

Male and female refugees alike confronted difficult problems in England and Canada—finding housing, obtaining financial support, settling into a new environment. For women, especially widows with families, the difficulties were compounded. The Bostonian Hannah Winslow found the right words: it was a "cruell" truth, she told her sister-in-law, that "when a woman with a family, and Particularly a large one, looses her Husband and Protector People are afraid to keep up the Acquaintance least they may ask favrs." Many of the men quickly reestablished their American friendship networks through the coffeehouses and refugee organizations; the women were deprived not only of the companionship such associations provided but also of the information about pensions and claims that was transmitted along the male networks. As a result, a higher proportion of female than male loyalists made errors in their applications for government assistance, by directing the memorials to the wrong officials

and failing to meet deadlines, often because they learned too late about compensation programs. Their standard excuses—that they "had nobody to advise with" and that they "did not know how to do it"—were greeted with skepticism by the claims commission, but they were undoubtedly true.

On the whole, female loyalists appear to have fared worse in England than their male counterparts, and for two major reasons. In the first place, the commissioners usually gave women annual pensions that were from £10 to £20 lower than those received by men, apparently because they believed that the women had fewer expenses, but also because in most cases the women could not claim the extra merit of having actively served the royal cause. Second, fewer women than men found work to supplement the sums they received from the government. To the wealthier female refugees work seemed so automatically foreclosed as an option that only a small number thought it necessary to explain to the commission why they could not contribute to their own support. Mary Serjeant, the widow of a Massachusetts clergyman, even regarded her former affluence as a sufficient reason in itself for her failure to seek employment. In 1782 she told the commissioners, "Educated as a Gentlewoman myself and brought up to no business I submit it to your [torn], Gentlemen, how very scanty must be that Subsistence which my Own Industry [can] procure us." Those who did try to earn additional income (many of whom had also worked outside the home in America) usually took in needlework or hired out as servants or housekeepers, but even they had trouble making ends meet. One orphaned young woman reported, "I can support myself with my needle: but not my two Sisters and infant Brother"; and another, who learned the trade of mantua making commented, "I now got Work for my self [sic]—but being oblidged to give long credit and haveing no Money of my one [sic] to go on with, I lived Chiefly upon tea which with night working brought me almost into the last stadge of a Consumtion so that when I rec'd my Money for work it went almost [all] to dockters."

Many of the loyalist women displayed a good deal of resilience. Some managed to support themselves, among them the Wells sisters of Charleston, who in 1789 opened a London boardinghouse for young ladies whose parents wished them to have a "suitable" introduction to society. Others survived what might seem an overwhelming series of setbacks—for example, Susannah Marshall of Maryland, who, after running taverns in Baltimore and Head of Elk and trying but failing to join Lord Dunmore off Norfolk in 1776, finally left the United States by sea the following year, only to have her chartered ship captured first by the Americans and then by the British. In the process she lost all the goods she had managed to salvage from her earlier moves, and when she arrived in England she not only learned of her husband's death but was unsuccessful in her application for a subsistence pension. Refusing to give up, she went to work as a nurse to support her children, and although she described herself to the commission in 1785 as "very Old and feeble," she

lived long enough to be granted a permanent annual allowance of £20 in 1789.

Susannah Marshall, though, had years of experience as a tavernkeeper behind her and was thus more capable of coping with her myriad difficulties than were women whose prewar experience had been restricted to their households. Such women recognized that they were "less able than many who never knew happier days to bear hardships and struggle with adversity." These women, especially those who had been, as one of them put it, *"born to better expectations"* in America, spoke despairingly of encounters with "difficultys of which she had no experience in her former life," of "Adversities which not many years before she scarcely thought it possible, that in any situation, she should ever experience."

For women like these, exile in England or Canada was one long nightmare. Their relief requests have a desperate, supplicating tone that is largely absent from those submitted by men. One bewailed the impending birth of her third child, asking, "What can I do in my Condishtion deprived of helth with our Friends or mony with a helpless family to suffer with me?" Another begged the commission's secretary for assistance "with all humility" because "the merciless man I lodge with, threatens to sell the two or three trifling articles I have and put a Padlock on the Room unless I pay him the Rent amounting to near a Pound." By contrast, when a man prepared a memorial for the exceptionally distressed Mrs. Sarah Baker, he coolly told the commissioners that they should assist her because her children "as Soldiers or Sailors in his Majesty's Service may in future compensate the present Expence of saving them."

The straits to which some of the female refugees were driven were dramatically illustrated in early 1783 when a South Carolina woman appeared before the commission "in Rags," explaining that she had been "obliged to pawn her Goods." It was but the first incident of many. Time and again women revealed that they had sold or pawned their clothes—which were usually their most valuable possessions—to buy food for themselves and their children. One was literally "reduced to the last shift" when she testified before the commission; another, the New Yorker Alicia Young, pawned so much that "the want of our apparel made our situation very deplorable" until friends helped her to redeem some of her possessions. Strikingly, no man ever told the commission stories like these. Either male refugees were able to find alternatives to pawning their clothes, or, if they did not, they were too ashamed to admit it.

Such hardships took a terrible mental as well as physical toll. Evidence of extreme mental stress permeates the female loyalists' petitions and letters, while it is largely absent from the memorials of male exiles. The women speak constantly of their "Fear, Fatigue and Anxiety of Mind," their "lowness of Spirit," their "inexpressable" distress, their "accumulated anguish." They repeatedly describe themselves as "desolate and distressed," as "disconsolate, Distressed and helpless . . . with a broken Spirit Ruined health and Constitution," as "Oppressed in body and distressed in mind." "I am

overwhelm'd with misfortunes," wrote one. Poverty "distracts and terrifies me," said another; and a third begged "that she may not be left a Prey to Poverty, and her constant companions [*sic*], Calamity and Sorrow." "My pen is unable to describe the horrors of My Mind—or the deploreable Situation of Myself and Infant family," Alicia Young told a member of the commission. "Judge then Dr Sir what is to become of me, or what we are to exist upon—I have no kind of resource . . . . oh Sir the horrors of my Situation is almost too much for me to bear." Most revealing of all was the wife of a Connecticut refugee: "Nature it self languishes," Mary Taylor wrote, "the hours that I should rest, I awake in such an aggitation of mind, as though I had to suffer for sins, that I neaver committed, I allmost shudder when I approache the Doone [doom?]—as every thing appears to be conspired against me, the Baker, and Bucher, seems to be weary of serving me oh porvity what is its Crime, may some have Compassion on those who feeals its power—for I can doo nothing—but baith my infant with my tears—while seeing my Husbands sinking under the waight of his misfortuens, unable to afford me any release.

Even taking into account the likelihood that it was more socially acceptable for women to reveal their emotions, the divergence between men's and women's memorials is too marked to be explained by that factor alone. It is necessary to probe more deeply and to examine men's and women's varying uses of language in order to delineate the full dimensions of the difference. As C. Wright Mills pointed out in an influential article some years ago, actions or motives and the vocabularies utilized to describe them cannot be wholly separated, and commonly used adjectives can therefore reveal the limitations placed on one's actions by one's social role. Mills asserted that "the 'Real Attitude or Motive' is not something different in kind from the verbalization or the 'opinion,' " and that "the long acting out of a role, with its appropriate motives, will often induce a man [or, one is compelled to add, a woman] to become what at first he merely sought to appear." Furthermore, Mills noted, people perceive situations in terms of specific, "delimited" vocabularies, and thus adjectives can themselves promote or deter certain actions. When adjectives are "typical and relatively unquestioned accompaniments of typal situations," he concluded, "such words often function as directives and incentives by virtue of their being the judgements of others as anticipated by the actor."

In this theoretical context the specific words used by female loyalists may be analyzed as a means of understanding the ways in which they perceived themselves and their circumstances. Their very phraseology—and the manner in which it differs from that of their male counterparts—can provide insights into the matrix of attitudes that helped to shape the way they thought and acted. If Mills is correct, the question whether the women were deliberately telling the commission what they thought it wanted to hear becomes irrelevant: it is enough to say that they were acting in accordance with a prescribed role, and that that role helped to determine how they acted.

With these observations in mind, the fact that the women refugees displayed an intense awareness of their own femininity assumes a crucial significance. The phrases permeate the pages of the petitions from rich and poor alike: "Though a Woman"; "perhaps no Woman in America in equal Circumstances"; "being done by a Woman"; "being a poor lame and infirm Woman." In short, in the female loyalists' minds their actions and abilities were to a certain extent defined by their sex. Femininity was the constant point of reference in measuring their achievements and making their self-assessments. Moreover, the fact of their womanhood was used in a deprecating sense. In their own eyes, they gained merit by not acting like women. Her services were "allmost Matchless, (being done by a Woman)," wrote one; "tho' a Woman, she was the first that went out of the Gates to welcome the Royal Army," declared another. Femininity also provided a ready and plausible excuse for failures of action or of knowledge. A South Carolinian said she had not signed the address to the king in Charleston in 1780 because "it was not posable for a woman to come near the office." A Pennsylvanian apologized for any errors in her loss estimate with the comment, "as far as a Woman can know, she believes the contents to be true." A Nova Scotian said she had not submitted a claim by the deadline because of "being a lone Woman in her Husband's Absence and not having any person to Advise with." A Vermonter made the ultimate argument: "had she been a man, Instead, of a poor helpless woman—should not have faild of being in the British Servace."

The pervasive implication is one of perceived inferiority, and this implication is enhanced by the word women used most often to describe themselves: "helpless." "Being a Poor helpless Widow"; "she is left a helpless Widow"; "a helpless woman advanced in life"; "being a helpless woman"; such phrases appear again and again in the claims memorials. Male loyalists might term themselves "very unhappy," "wretched," "extremely distressed," or "exceedingly embarrassed," but *never* were they "helpless." For them, the most characteristic self-description was "unfortunate," a word that carried entirely different, even contrary, connotations. Male loyalists can be said to have seen their circumstances as not of their own making, as even being reversible with luck. The condition of women, however, was inherent in themselves; nothing they could do could change their circumstances. By definition, indeed, they were incapable of helping themselves.

It should be stressed here that, although women commonly described themselves as "helpless," their use of that word did not necessarily mean that they were in fact helpless. It indicates rather that they perceived thus, and that that perception in turn perhaps affected the way they acted (for example, in seeking charitable support instead of looking for work). Similarly, the fact that men failed to utilize the adjective "helpless" to refer to themselves does not mean that they were not helpless, for some of them surely were; it merely shows that— however incorrectly—they did think that they could change their circumstances. These two words, with all their connotations, encapsulate much of the divergence between male and female self-perceptions in late eighteenth-century America, even if they do not necessarily indicate much about the realities of male-female relationships in the colonies.

There was, of course, more to the difference in sex roles than the sex-related ways in which colonial Americans looked at themselves. The claims documents also suggest that women and men placed varying emphases on familial ties. For women, such relationships seemed to take on a special order of magnitude. Specifically, men never said, as several women did, that after their spouses' deaths they were so "inconsolable" that they were unable to function. One woman declared that after her husband's execution by the rebels she was "bereft of her reason for near three months," and another described herself as "rendered almost totally incapable of Even writing my own Name or any assistance in any Shape that Could have the least Tendency to getting my Bread." Furthermore, although loyalist men expressed concern over the plight of the Children they could not support adequately, women were much more emotionally involved in the fate of their offspring. "Your goodness will easily conceive, what I must feel for My *Children*," Alicia Young told a claims commissioner; "for myself— I care not—Misfortunes and distress have long since made me totally indifferent to everything in the World but *Them*—they have no provision—no provider—no protector—but God—and me." Women noted that their "Sorrows" were increased by the knowledge that their children were "Partners in this Scene of Indigence."

Margaret Draper, widow of a Boston printer, explained that although she had been ill and suffering from a "disorderd Mind," "what adds to my affliction is, my fears for my Daughter, who may soon be left a Stranger and friendless." In the same vein, a New Jersey woman commented that she had "the inexpressible mortification of seeing my Children in want of many necessaries and conveniencies . . . and what still more distresses me, is to think that I am obliged by partaking of it, to lessen even the small portion they have."

The women's emphasis on their families is entirely compatible with the earlier observation concerning the importance of their households in their lives. If their menfolk were preoccupied with the monetary consequences of adhering to the crown, the women were more aware of the human tragedy brought about by the war. They saw their plight and that of their children in much more personal terms than did their husbands. Likewise, they personalized the fact of their exile in a way that male loyalists did not, by almost invariably commenting that they were "left friendless in a strange Country." Refugee men, though they might call themselves "strangers," rarely noted a lack of friends, perhaps because of the coffeehouse networks. To women, by contrast, the fact that they were not surrounded by friends and neighbors seemed calamitous. "I am without Friends or Money," declared one; I am "a friendless, forlorn Woman . . . a Stranger to this Country, and surrounded by evils," said another. She is "far from her native Country, and numerous Friends and Relations where she formerly lived, much respected,"

she formerly lived, much respected," wrote a third of her own condition.

When the female refugees talked of settling elsewhere or of returning to the United States, they spoke chiefly of the friends and relatives they would find at their intended destinations. Indeed, it appears from the claims that at least six women went into exile solely because their friends and relatives did. A loyalist woman who remained in the United States after the war explained that she did so because she chose "to reside near my relations [rather] than to carry my family to a strange Country where in case of my death they would be at the mercy of strangers." And Mary Serjeant's description of her situation in America as it would have been had her husband not been a loyalist carried the implication that she wished she too had stayed at home: "His poor Children and disconsolate Widow would now have had a House of their own and some Land adjoining to it And instead of being almost destitute in a Land of Strangers would have remained among some Relatives."

In sum, evidence drawn from the loyalist claims strongly suggests that late-eighteenth-century women had fully internalized the roles laid out for them in the polite literature of the day. Their experience was largely confined to their households, either because they chose that course or because they were forced into it. They perceived themselves as "helpless"—even if at times their actions showed that they were not—and they strongly valued ties with family and friends. When the Revolution tore them from the familiar patterns of their lives in America, they felt abandoned and adrift, far more so than did their male relatives, for whom the human contacts cherished by the women seemed to mean less or at least were more easily replaced by those friendships that persisted into exile.

The picture of the late-eighteenth-century woman that emerges from the loyalist claims, therefore, is of one who was almost wholly domestic, in the sense that that word would be used in the nineteenth-century United States. But at the same time the co-lonial woman's image of herself lacked the positive attributes with which her nineteenth-century counterpart could presumably console herself. The eighteenth-century American woman was primarily a wife and a mother, but America had not yet developed an ideology that would proclaim the social value of motherhood. That was to come with republicanism—and loyalist women, by a final irony, were excluded by their political allegiance from that republican assurance.

# The Exclusion of the Loyalists

WILLIAM H. NELSON (b. 1923) has been opposed to the arbitrary categorization of loyalists or "tories" simply as those colonials who remained politically attached to Great Britain. For many, he argued in *The American Tory*, adherence to Britain was merely a byproduct of their disagreement with other Americans over the kind of institutions the provinces should have and the kind of society America should be. Nelson claims that the loyalist ranks were composed of all types of colonists, but that they all had one thing in common: they were all members of conscious minorities in the regions where they lived. They also felt weak or threatened in one way or another, and were more afraid of an independent America than they were of continued allegiance to Great Britain. But why did loyalists not think in terms of a conspiracy to destroy American liberties, as described by Professor Bailyn? Why was their worldview different? How were their fears reflected in the nature of the Revolutionary experience?

# The Tory Rank and File

It is not surprising that the role of the Tories in the American Revolution has been misunderstood persistently. The Tories themselves were confused about their essential position. Because they came eventually to regard their loyalty to Britain as their own primary political characteristic; because they called themselves Loyalists and forgot they had been Tories first, they have naturally perplexed historians. To see the Tories only as people who remained attached politically to Britain is, however, to distort their outlook and to ignore the necessities of their case. For many of them, adherence to Britain was, at the time, only an incident in their battle with other Americans over what kind of institutions America ought to have. For these people it was less a matter of staying with Britain, than of being left with Britain by the fortunes of war and the intensity of political rancour. Like all civil wars, the American Revolution was of slow growth. The Loyalists, like the revolutionists, were grouped together and were sent marching down a road of no return by a very gradual polarization of colonial society. . . .

Years before the Revolution a number of men who were to be the Loyalist leaders were attempting to use British authority to establish and fortify local oligarchies in the colonies. It is true that these people usually thought of their political ideal as aristocratic, but it was necessarily oligarchic, given the absence in America and decay in England of a genuine aristocratic tradition. As Jonathan Boucher wrote, a little regretfully: 'In the present state of human affairs, . . . a man has, or has not, influence, only as he has, or has not, the power of conferring favours.' The only patronage the American Tories could use was that of the Crown, and the Tory vanguard was made up of people whose attachment to, or dependence on, the British government was direct. These men included most of the royal office-holders: the governors, many of the provincial councillors and judges, the customs officials, Indian agents, and various lesser placemen. It also included the Anglican clergy in the Northern Colonies where the Church depended directly on British support. And the Tory leaders included a few politicians like Joseph Galloway and William Smith, men who were not office-holders, but whose fears or ambitions led them in an imperial rather than a national direction.

Here it is important to observe that what distinguished these men from other American leaders was not primarily their oligarchic outlook. For this they shared with most of the men who were to lead the Revolution and write the constitution. The notion that in a well-ordered society political power ought to be in the hands of a wise and wealthy minority was held by all kinds of good Whigs. What distinguished the Tory from the Whig oligarchs was that the former needed, and the latter did not need, support from Britain, since the Whig oligarchs could, and the Tories could not, gain sufficient support in America to hold power. The basic weakness of the Tories was not their attachment to Britain, for this was a consequence of their weakness; rather their weakness lay in the fact that they held social or political opinions which could prevail in America only with British assistance.

In the period between 1750 and 1770 there were several Tory projects requiring the help of the British government. The Anglican clergy in the North were working for the establishment of an American episcopate and for further government favours for their Church. In Pennsylvania the Anti-Proprietary party was trying to get Pennsylvania made a royal province in order to consolidate the power of the Philadelphia mercantile community. In all the colonies there were groups of ambitious politicians who had chosen office-holding under the Crown as the way to power or prestige. With the growing complexity of government in America there was a steady increase in the number of places available to such men. Some, like Thomas Hutchinson in Massachusetts and John Wentworth in New Hampshire, were on the way to becoming royal governors. . . .

It is clear that one obvious handicap the Tories were to suffer in attempting to uphold British authority was their own distaste for the measures being pursued by the British government, and their sympathy for what at first appeared to be an American rather than a revolutionary cause. This embarrassment undoubtedly accounts in part for the comparative scarcity of Tory arguments in the 1760's. Even as early as the time of the Stamp Act, however, a few suspicious Tories began, not to defend British taxation of America, but to question the ends and means of the more violent American critics of Parliament. . . .

Looking back on this period after the Revolution, most of the Tory writers were able to see a regular progression of events leading inevitably to revolution and independence. This seeming inevitability was a product of afterthought, however, since events as they happened did not possess the clarity they acquired in retrospect. At the time most of the Tories yielded to the common temptation of those who are satisfied with things as they are, to expect things to remain as they are. Like most anti-revolutionists, they found it difficult to regard the mere threat of revolution seriously. Thus at almost any time between 1765 and 1774 it seemed to most of them that the revolutionary movement had nearly run its course, and that matters would shortly be as they had been before the Stamp Act.

Even when they were sure of their cause and sure that it needed their advocacy, the Tories were comparatively ineffective advocates. They could not compete with the Whigs in organization, and they did not try to compete as propagandists. They distrusted innovations and were sceptical about reforms, so that while, in idle moments, many of them speculated on the constitutional problems facing the colonies, they failed utterly, during the years when they might have been

listened to, to suggest a reasonable alternative to revolution. Apart from Galloway's plan for a union with Britain, discussed in a leisurely and academic way in Philadelphia, the Tory leaders avoided the basic issues of constitutional reform, and concentrated their attention on minor and peripheral matters: the need for more (or fewer) British troops, or for higher salaries for judges, or for restrictions against town meetings. Most of the Tory office-holders seem to have been incapable of seeing beneath the superficial problems of administrative reform to the basic problems of constitutional reform.

Not only did they not develop and proclaim an agreed alternative to revolution, the Tories did not even consult among themselves except in the most haphazard and informal way. They developed no Committees of Correspondence, and very little political correspondence at all. Their letters remained the desultory and amiable communications of complacent gentle-folk. In fact, except for the Anglican parsons, the principal Tories in the different provinces, men like Hutchinson in Massachusetts, and Galloway in Pennsylvania, did not even know each other. It is odd to find some of them recording their first impressions of each other, in exile in London, long after the debate was over and their day was done.

Most of all, the Tories were simply unable to cultivate public opinion, to form it and inform it. They showed not a trace of the skill with which, for example, Samuel Adams learned in these years to involve the reading public and the local politicians in a reciprocal catechism of alarms and grievances, of petitions and manifestoes echoed interminably back and forth, from committee to assembly, from assembly to committee, from the press to the public to the press. The Tories were, in fact, afraid of public opinion, afraid of men gathered together, even symbolically, in large numbers. They were afraid, for they felt weak. Here indeed is to be found the basic Tory inhibition during these years of argument, the real and compelling excuse for their apathy. They had ideas, beliefs, values, interests which they were afraid to submit to an American public for approval or rejection. And the weaker they felt themselves to be, the tighter became their allegiance to Britain. The closer they were bound to Britain, the less able were they to support effectively her cause or theirs. So, as the American quarrel with the British government grew more bitter and more deadly, the Tories began slowly, under the guise of loyalty, to sink into a helpless dependence on Britain, an attachment no longer voluntary but growing desperate, and as it became desperate, ceasing to be quite honourable. . . .

In the folk tales of nineteenth-century America, two kinds of Loyalists were remembered, presumably because a certain romantic interest clung to them. There were the Tory gentlefolk, Royalists who lived in great houses and drove about in fine carriages; and there were fearful outlaws who, in these remembrances, generally travelled with Indians—'Tories and Indians'. With the disappearance of the frontier and the Indians, the outlaw Tories were forgotten, and historians, in attempting to rationalize the legends of a Tory gentry, slipped into an easy explanation of the Revolution in class terms. By this account, the Tories were either frightened or selfish oligarchs, who had fought the Revolution in order to protect their special privileges. Although traces of this view still survive, more recent students have emphasized the dangers of making class generalizations about the Revolution.

Certainly there are a woeful number of exceptions to any generalizations that may be made about the Loyalists. Besides, at first glance, there seems little useful that might be said in the same breath about Governor Hutchinson, say, and a Carolina backwoodsmen; or about William Byrd of Westover, and a Brooklyn shopkeeper. Yet if the Tories are to be really understood, and if their dissent from a major decision of their countrymen is to be at all meaningful, an attempt must be made to set them in social rather than in merely individual terms. And it may be that in the very diversity of the Tory ranks there can be found a clue to the identity of the 'army'.

Of all the approaches that might be used in an attempt to separate intelligibly the Loyalists from their Patriot kinsmen, that of occupation or social class seems the least fruitful. There was indeed a Tory oligarchy, but there was also a Whig oligarchy, and if in New England the Tory proportion of ruling families was greater than the Tory proportion of the total population, in the Southern Colonies the reverse was true. Even in New England the Loyalists were hardly the gentry pictured in legend. When an Act of Banishment was passed against some three hundred Loyalists in Massachusetts in 1778, they were listed by trade or profession. About a third were merchants, professional men, and gentlemen; another third were farmers, and the rest were artisans or labourers with a sprinkling of small shopkeepers.

Most random lists of Loyalists show even less evidence of gentility than this. Always the gentlemen, esquires, merchants, and the like are far outnumbered by the yeomen, cordwainers, tailors, labourers, masons, blacksmiths, and their fellows. The social heterogeneity of the New York Tories is evident in the list of people arrested there in June 1776 on suspicion of plotting to assassinate General Washington. These people included the mayor of New York, some other officials and gentlemen, some farmers, several tavern-keepers, a shoemaker, two doctors, several apprentices and labourers, two tanners, a silversmith, a saddler, two gunsmiths, a tallow chandler, a miller, a schoolmaster, a former schoolmaster, a former constable, a 'pensioner with one arm,' and one unfortunate man described only as 'a damned rascal.'

Clearly, none of the simpler economic determinants was at work separating Whigs from Tories. Economic influences, however, may account in part for the pattern of geographical distribution that appears when the Loyalist strongholds are considered. The main centres of Tory strength fall into two distinct regions: The first was along the thinly settled western frontier, from Georgia and District Ninety-Six in South Carolina, through the Regulator country of North Carolina and the mountain settlements of Virginia, Pennsylvania, and New York, to the newly-occupied Vermont lands. The other was the maritime region of the Middle Colonies, including western Long Island and the counties of the lower Hudson Valley, southern New Jersey, the three old counties of Pennsylvania around Philadelphia, and the peninsula between Delaware and Chesapeake Bays. There were also locally important concentrations of Tories elsewhere along the Atlantic seaboard: at Charleston, around Wilmington and Norfolk, and around Newport and Portsmouth in New England.

In the West and in the tidal region of the Middle Colonies Loyalists and neutrals may have formed a majority of the population. In the areas of dense agricultural settlement, however, including the plantation country of the Southern Colonies, the thickly settled parts of the Piedmont, and most of New England, Loyalists were comparatively scarce. All that the Tory regions, the mountain and maritime frontiers, had in common was that both suffered or were threatened with economic and political subjugation by richer adjoining areas. The geographical concentration of the Tories was in peripheral areas, regions already in decline, or not yet risen to importance.

It is not difficult to explain the Loyalism of the West. The Appalachian frontiersmen—hunters, trappers, and fur traders—feared the advance of close settlement would destroy their economy. Like the Indians of the region, many of the frontiersmen were loyal to Britain because the British government was the only force they could rely on to check the rapid advance of agricultural settlement. The tidal region of the Middle Colonies, on the other hand, still had political power, but was in danger of losing it to the more populous districts inland. Moreover, this region formed part of an Atlantic community. It looked east-ward; its ties with Britain were closer than its ties with the new West. Even in New England the truly maritime regions seem to have been less than enthusiastic in their support of the Revolution. Newport lacked zeal; Nantucket and Martha's Vineyard were opportunist or neutral, and the Maine coast grew steadily less faithful to the Revolution, until Nova Scotia's Loyalism of necessity was reached.

Whether the St. Lawrence Valley should be considered a separate province, or whether it merely combined the characteristics of a thinly settled and a maritime region, it too was indifferent or hostile to the Revolution. Undoubtedly some of Vermont's capriciousness during the period may be ascribed to the pull of the St. Lawrence. In any case, wherever regions newly or thinly settled touched the sea, there the Revolution was weakest: in Quebec, in Nova Scotia, in Georgia, and in New York where the Hudson carried the Atlantic world into the mountains. Wherever sailors and fishermen, trappers and traders outnumbered farmers and planters, there Tories outnumbered Whigs.

Of course a major insufficiency of such a geographical analysis is that it takes no account of important cultural influences, differences in nationality and religion mainly, that played a great role in the Revolution. The Canadians of the St. Lawrence Valley were suspicious of the Revolution, not only because they lived far outside its physical homeland, but also because they were French and Catholic, and the Revolution seemed to them English and Protestant. No geographic or economic considerations can explain

the Tory villages on Long Island, intermingled with Whig villages. The Tory villages were Dutch, while the others had been settled by New Englanders. Here again, legend has done a disservice to students of the Revolution. The Loyalists were seldom more English than the patriots. There were, of course, many British-born Tories whose allegiance to England was habitual and natural. But, apart from these, the Tories more commonly drew their recruits from the non-English than from the English parts of the community. The two most purely English provinces, Virginia and Massachusetts, were the strongholds of the Revolution. It was in the patchwork societies of Pennsylvania and New York that the Tories were strongest.

Among almost all cultural minorities, the proportion of Tories seems to have been clearly higher than among the population at large. The Dutch and Germans seem to have inclined towards supporting the Revolution where they were already anglicized, but not where they had kept their language and separate outlook. In New York, for example, the English-speaking Dutch Reformed congregation was Whiggish, but the Dutch-speaking congregation was Tory, and on such cordial terms with the Anglicans that they were allowed to use St. George's chapel during the British occupation. The Tories praised the loyalty of the French Calvinists at New Rochelle, the only place in the colonies where they had preserved their language, while elsewhere the descendants of the Huguenots were conspicuously active revolutionists.

There seems to have been reason for John Witherspoon's lament that his fellow Scots made bad revolutionists, whether Highlanders in the back country of New York and North Carolina, or Lowlanders along the Virginia and Carolina coast. Even the Ulstermen were tainted with Toryism in the Regulator districts of North Carolina and in the frontier districts of South Carolina. The Loyalism of the Indians is well known, and contemporary opinion held that the Negroes were dangerously Toryfied. Of course people like the Brooklyn Dutch or the South Carolina Germans and Scots may have remained loyal to Britain partly out of political quietism. It is difficult not to believe, however, that they were Loyalists also because they thought Britain would protect them from the cultural aggression of an Anglo-American majority.

In religion, the lines that divided Tories from Whigs were quite clearly drawn. Adherents of religious groups that were in a local minority were everywhere inclined towards Loyalism, while adherents of the dominant local denomination were most often Patriots. In New England not many Congregationalists, in the Middle Colonies not many Presbyterians, in the South not many Episcopalians, were Tories. Conversely, most of the Anglicans in the North were Tories; so were many Presbyterians in the Episcopalian South. Of the smaller religious groups, most of the Quakers and German Pietists were passive Loyalists, and in New England even the Baptists were accused of 'not being hearty' in the American cause. The reputation the Methodists had for being poor rebels was perhaps not entirely due to the influence of Wesley and other English ministers. The Catholics and Jews apparently form an exception to the rule that religious minorities leaned towards Toryism. Both seem generally to have supported the Revolution, although among the Jews there were notable exceptions like the Hart family in Newport and the Franks family in Philadelphia. Jonathan Boucher observed that although the Maryland Catholics supported the Revolution in its later stages, they had taken little part at first. It is possible that the Jews and Catholics were in such suspect and habitual minority, that they felt obliged to follow what seemed majority opinion for their own safety.

Taking all the groups and factions, sects, classes, and inhabitants of regions that seem to have been Tory, they have but one thing in common: they represented conscious minorities, people who felt weak and threatened. The sense of weakness, which is so marked a characteristic of the Tory leaders, is equally evident among the rank and file. Almost all the Loyalists were, in one way or another, more afraid of America than they were of Britain. Almost all of them had interests that they felt needed protection from an American majority. Being fairly certain that they would be in a permanent minority (as Quakers or oligarchs or frontiersmen or Dutchmen) they could not find much comfort in a theory of government that assured them of sovereign equality with other Americans *as individuals*. Not many Loyalists were as explicit in their distrust of individualism as, say, Jonathan Boucher, but most of them shared his suspicion of a political order based on the 'common good' if the common good was to be defined by a numerical majority.

A theory that the Loyalists were compounded of an assortment of minority groups does not, of course, preclude their having in total constituted a majority of Americans. Without the social and religious homogeneity, without the common purpose, and without the organic and efficient leadership of the revolutionists, the Loyalists might still have outnumbered them. In this case the Revolution would have been, as it has sometimes been claimed to have been, the achievement of an organized and wilful minority. The problem of discovering how many Tories there were is complicated, moreover, by there having been, between avowed supporters and avowed opponents of the Revolution, a great middle group of passive citizens who had no clear point of view, who hoped perhaps that one side or the other would win, but who wanted above all not to be disturbed. There must have been many like the New Jersey shopkeeper who stood in his door and prayed that whatever happened, he might have peace in his time. There were probably also a good number of sceptics who thought as John Ross of Philadelphia did: 'Let who would be king, he well knew that he should be subject.'

An old and symmetrical guess that a third of Americans were revolutionists, another third Loyalists, and a third neutral, has long been accepted by historians as reasonable. It goes back, presumably, to John Adams's assignment of these relative proportions. But Adams may have been trying, unconsciously, to gain distinction for the revolutionists by maintaining they were a wise minority. . . . A more reasonable guess than Adams's would be that the Loyalists were a third, and the revolutionists two-thirds of the politically active population of the colonies.

WALLACE BROWN (b. 1933) demonstrates in this excerpt from *The Good Americans: The Loyalists in the American Revolution,* that the loyalists had good reason to be afraid of other Americans. Not only did they often lose their property, their legal rights, and their ability to make their livings, but they also frequently suffered cruel separation from family and friends. In spite of the fact that there were neither guillotines nor mass executions in the American as compared with the French Revolution, Brown points out that selective forms of terror abetted the rebels' cause. Does the intolerance shown loyalists help explain the extent of the achievements and failures of the American Revolution? Was intolerance an inhibiting factor which spilled over into other areas? Would it have been possible to have a successful revolution without stifling the loyalists? How should students interpret the Revolution and its impact on the people, when it used terror against some while developing republican institutions for others?

# "Damn the Tories": Persecution

"The Cry was for Liberty—Lord, what a Fuss!
But pray, how much liberty left they for us?"
*Anonymous, Loyalist Rhapsodies.*

What might be called official or semi-official action (it was hardly legal until July 4, 1776) against the Loyalists began with the adoption of the Continential Association by the Congress in 1774 and continued with the work of various local committees and the colonial, and then state, legislatures. During the period of the Revolutionary War a great jumble of legislation was passed by the thirteen states, with some superfluous goading from the Congress, and the result was that the disabilities suffered by Loyalists varied a great deal.

All states passed at least one test law requiring inhabitants to take oaths, which usually involved abjuring George III and pledging allegiance to the new regime and faith in the Revolution.

Categories of persons to whom the laws applied varied, but commonly included all adult males. Penalties for refusal included suspension from office, imprisonment, disfranchisement, barring from political office, withdrawal of legal rights, extra taxation, confiscation of property, banishment, and execution if any exiles should return. Many took the oaths demanded by one side or the other hypocritically, and, of course, the number of adherents to each side waxed and waned with the fortunes of war. There were many other commonly found laws concerning the Loyalists that contained provisions for billeting troops with them, forcing them to accept payments in Continental paper money, levying fines of increasing severity for refusal to serve in the militia and for many other unpatriotic actions, restricting their freedom by censorship of speech and action, disfranchising them and barring them from office and from the legal and the teaching professions, exiling them to another part of the state, to another state altogether, or from the whole United States. The shifting of dangerous Loyalists to Whiggish areas was common, especially when a place was threatened militarily. Thus Rhode Island sent some of its Loyalists to the northern part of the state, and Connecticut received New York and New Jersey Loyalists. As early as 1777 every state save South Carolina and Georgia had made traitors of all who actively supported the British. The celebrated Pennsylvania "Black List" of 490 Loyalists attainted of high treason was made up largely of men who had left with the British forces. In the end a few were pardoned and several were executed.

In November, 1777, the Continental Congress recommended the confiscation of Loyalist estates, a suggestion already made by Thomas Paine, and in some places already acted upon. All states finally amerced, taxed, or confiscated much Loyalist property, and in addition New York and South Carolina taxed Loyalist property in order to compensate robbery victims. Some towns simply raffled off Tory property. Patriot officers requisitioned horses and supplies from Loyalists rather than Whigs, and, of course, there was much old-fashioned looting, particularly of the property of exiles. Like Henry VII's dissolution of the monasteries, the disbursement of Loyalist property created a vested interest in revolution. Also the device of trying partially to finance the war with traitors' wealth was naturally very popular, if of limited success. Many Whigs, some of them racketeers, did very well by taking the advice of an Albany, New York, merchant who wrote: "I find myself justified by Experience in declaring that a judicious Purchase of forfeited Lands . . . is by far the most Eligible mode I know of Improving a Fortune in a Secure way." One observer thought it common for Loyalist estates to sell for less than one quarter of their real value. . . .

A myriad of particularities could play a part in determining the extent of persecution. A well-liked or respected Tory (and there were a few such) might well escape, as might someone whose skills were especially valued, for example, a doctor. Influential but quiet Loyalists were more apt to avoid penalties than those of lower social standing or those more vociferous in their beliefs.

The zeal of the patriots could be extremely capricious and, as always with witch-hunts, frequently ridiculous and heavy-handed. One citizen was accosted for naming his dog "Tory," the implication being that a Tory was forced to lead a dog's life. In 1776 at Stratford, Connecticut, an Episcopal minister was brought before the local committee because he had officiated at a baptism where the child was named Thomas Gage. The committee viewed the action as a "designed insult" and censured the cleric. In the same state Zephaniah Beardslee reported that he was "very much abused" for naming his daughter Charlotte, after the queen. It may be noted that Beardslee, apparently a very serious Loyalist, had also been found drinking the king's health. The frequent persecution of Tories for this activity, however, is not as picayune as it seems, because toasts presuppose groups in taverns and the chance of Loyalist plots and associations. Thus, Abraham Cuyler held a gathering in Albany, New York, in June, 1776, that featured drinking and the singing of "God Save the King." At last the enraged Whig citizens crashed the party and carried the royal merrymakers off to jail.

Frequently old scores were settled or the unpopular chastised under cover of patriot enthusiasm. Crèvecoeur had a Whig explain: "This great land of Canaan cannot be purged of its ancient idolaters without abundance of trouble. Now the Jews had a much better chance because the Canaanites did not speak the same language. We must guess, and sift, and find out; no wonder if we make mistakes sometimes." James Simpson summed things up rather well and gave an interesting example of the vagaries of circumstances:

It is notorious that the conduct of the Americans, in proscribing the persons, and confiscating the Estates of their fellow Citizens, have been very little influenced by the rules of indiscriminate Justice, or strict Impartiality, a considerable Property, hath frequently been the cause of condemnation, but hath sometimes been the means of Salvation to the Owners of it, for when a person of extensive influence had a prospect or perhaps a certainty of a rich succession he would of course use his endeavors to prevent a measure which would destroy his expectations.

The Loyalists suffered in many ways that were not the direct results of legislation or government action. For example, they were often required to illuminate their houses (an action forced on recalcitrants in England by the Wilkes mobs of the 1760's) to celebrate such an event as an American military victory. Many social pressures were brought to bear, admittedly given encouragement (normally superfluous) by various legal or semilegal bodies. Thus a committee at Skenesborough, New York, published the name of a citizen who had opposed the Continental Association, announcing that "[we] hereby give notice to the public that he may be treated with all that neglect and contempt which is so justly his due, for his incorrigible enmity to the rights of American Liberty."

The results of Loyalism might simply be social ostracism—being sent to Coventry—as, for instance, happened to James Allen, who noted in his diary for February 17, 1777: "I never knew how painful it is to be secluded from the free conversation of one's friends"; and to George Watson, a mandamus councillor, when he entered a church at Plymouth, Massachusetts, and "a great number of the principal inhabitants left." Or it might mean serious loss of services, as when the blacksmiths of Worcester County, Massachusetts, refused to work for any Loyalists, their employees, or their dependents; or an economic boycott, as in Connecticut, where the local committee forbade "all Persons whatever viz. Merchants Mechanicks Millers and Butchers and Co. from supplying . . . John Sayre or Family with any manner of Thing whatever." Lawyers, teachers, doctors, apothecaries, and others often lost their customers and hence their livelihoods. Mathew Robinson, a Newport trader, from the first branded as "a Rank Torey," suffered several indignities, including the pulling down of his fences by a "multitude . . . under colour of laying out a Highway" and climaxing in 1781 when, after *"a New England Saint"* charged that Robinson "drank the King's Health, and damn'd the Congress and call'd them damn'd Rebels and Presbyterians," he was imprisoned by the rebels without examination, this being even "against their own Bill of Rights."

In many areas—for example, New York—the Loyalists were allowed to sell their property before departing, but such hurried, desperate sales were unlikely to net a fair price, and the result amounted to confiscation.

All wars and revolutions cause great mental strain and suffering, most of which goes unmeasured. The history of the Revolutionary era is liberally punctuated with stories of Loyalists who succumbed to melancholia, became mad, died, or committed suicide. Alexander Harvey, a Charleston law-yer, wound up in a private English madhouse, having been "driven to Distraction" by his experiences as a Loyalist; George Miller, a North Carolina merchant whose fright had conquered his Loyalist principles, was thrown "into Convulsions" by the strain of serving in the American militia; Peter Harrison's death came after the shock of Lexington, and with it America lost its greatest colonial architect; several Loyalists, including the wife of William Franklin, simply died of "a Broken Heart"; the widow of Dr. Robert Gibbs of South Carolina recounted that the prospect of the loss of his property "so preyed upon his Spirits" that he died. Andrew Miller, of Halifax, North Carolina, was estranged from all his friends by his Loyalism, which literally killed him; others chose suicide —Millington Lockwood of Connecticut was wounded in the head, lost his reason, and drowned himself, while some years later, in London, after years of fruitless waiting for compensation, an unnamed, ruined Loyalist shot himself in despair, blaming an ungrateful country.

Although Americans at the time of the Revolution would clearly have found it odd, today one of the sharpest historical debates is over the question of how far the American Revolution was a *real* revolution. Even those historians who, noting the social dislocation, argue that the American Revolution was rather like the French Revolution stress the absence of the Terror. Mass executions there were not, a guillotine there was not, yet atrocities and terror there most certainly were. It is fitting that in the beginning the rebels "hoisted the Red Flag or Flag of Defence."

Leaving aside civil war aspects such as the execution and maltreatment of prisoners and the burning of towns (by both sides: for example, the Americans fired Norfolk and Portsmouth; the British, Falmouth and Fairfield), we can cite a great range of fates that awaited the Loyalists; they were catalogued by "Papinian" as tarring and feathering, rail riding,

. . . chaining men together by the dozens, and driving them, like herds of cattle, into distant provinces, flinging them into loathesome jails, confiscating their estates, shooting them in swamps and woods as suspected Tories, hanging them after a mock trial; and all this because they would not abjure their rightful Sovereign, and bear arms against him.

Tarring and feathering (pine tar and goose feathers) became the classic Whig treatment of the Tories, and the British Government believed there was "no better proof of Loyalty" than suffering this punishment. A famous instance of it occurred in Boston on January 25, 1774, and is worth recounting in some detail.

At about eight o'clock in the evening a club-wielding mob milled along Cross Street. Their objective was John Malcolm, a distinguished but hot-tempered veteran of the French and Indian War, a native Bostonian, an ex-overseas merchant turned royal customs official, and a highly unpopular man for many reasons connected with both his personality (he was inordinately quarrelsome) and his job.

His recent arrival in Boston had been preceded by the unpopular news that in 1771 he had helped the governor of North Carolina against those reputedly Whiggish rebels known as the Regulators and that in October, 1773, he had officiously seized a brigantine at Falmouth (now Portland), Maine. Malcolm waited, ready and armed, behind barred doors. Undeterred, the mob raised ladders, broke an upstairs window, captured their prey, dragged him onto a sled, and pulled him along King Street to the Customs House, or Butcher's House, as it was popularly known, where the spectators gave three mighty cheers.

Although it was "one of the severest cold nights" of the winter, so cold that both Boston Harbor and even the very ink as it touched paper had frozen hard, the wretched man was put in a cart, stripped "to buff and breeches," and dealt the punishment of tarring and feathering, which American patriots were soon to convert into a major spectator sport. Malcolm, self-styled "Single Knight of the Tarr," as opposed to English Knights of the Garter, had already suffered the same indignity the year before for his conduct at Falmouth. He later claimed to be the first in America tarred for loyalty.

A contemporary description gives a good idea of how Malcolm and many others were treated:

The following is the Receipe for an effectual Operation. "First strip a Person naked, then heat the Tar until it is thin, and pour it upon the naked Flesh, or rub it over with a Tar Brush, *quantum sufficit*. After which, sprinkle decently upon the Tar, whilst it is yet warm, as many Feathers as will stick to it. Then hold a lighted Candle to the Feathers, and try to set it all on Fire; if it will burn so much the better. But as the Experiment is often made in cold Weather; it will not then succeed—take also an Halter and put it round the Person's Neck, and then cart him the Rounds."

Malcolm, flogged and otherwise molested at intervals, was paraded around various crowded streets with his neck in a halter and was finally taken to the Liberty Tree, where he refused to resign his royal office or to curse Thomas Hutchinson, the hated governor of Massachusetts.

The crowd then set off for the gallows on Boston Neck. On the way Malcolm gasped an affirmative when one of his tormentors asked if he was thirsty and was given a bowl of strong tea and ordered to drink the king's health. Malcolm was next told to drink the queen's health; then two more quarts of tea were produced with the command to drink to the health of the Prince of Wales.

"Make haste, you have nine more healths to drink," shouted one of the mob.

"For God's sake, Gentlemen, be merciful, I'm ready to burst; if I drink a drop more, I shall die," Malcolm implored.

"Suppose you do, you die in a good cause, and it is as well to be drowned as hanged," was the reply.

The nine healths, beginning with the "Bishop of Osnabrug," were forced down the victim's throat. Malcolm "turned pale, shook his Head, and instantly filled the Bowl which he had just emptied."

"What, are you sick of the royal family?"

"No, my stomach nauseates the tea; it rises at it like poison."

"And yet you rascal, your whole fraternity at the Custom House would drench us with this poison, and we are to have our throats cut if it will not stay upon our stomachs."

At the gallows the noose was placed in position around Malcolm's neck and he was threatened with hanging, but he still refused to submit, whereupon he was "basted" with a rope for a while, and finally, on pain of losing his ears, he gave in and cursed the governor. The stubborn, brave man was further carted around the town, made to repeat various humiliating oaths, and finally deposited back at his home just before midnight, half frozen, an arm dislocated, and, as he said, "in a most mizerable setuation Deprived of his senses." Five days later, bedridden and "terribly bruised," he dictated a complaint to Governor Hutchinson, which his injuries obliged him to sign with an *X*.

The frost and tar caused an infection that made his skin peel extensively. However, he was careful to preserve a piece of skin with the tar and feathers still adhering (the stuff was the very devil to get off), which he carried to England as proof of his sufferings when, somewhat recovered, he set sail on May 2, 1774, to try to gain compensation for his loyalty.

Another Tory punishment that became traditional was the gruesome riding on a rail that sometimes followed tarring and feathering, but was severe enough in itself. It consisted of jogging the victim roughly along on "a sharp rail" between his legs. The painful effect of these "grand Toory Rides," as a contemporary called them, can readily be imagined. Seth Seely, a Connecticut farmer, was brought before the local committee in 1776 and for signing a declaration to support the king's laws was "put on a Rail carried on mens Shoulders thro the Street, then put into the Stocks and besmeared with Eggs and was robbed of money for the Entertainment of the Company."

Persecution of the Loyalists came in many forms. In 1778 prisoners in Vermont were made to tread a road through the snow in the Green Mountains. The wife of Edward Brinley was pregnant and waiting out her confinement at Roxbury, Massachusetts, accompanied by "a guard of Rebels always in her room, who treated her with great rudeness and indecency, exposing her to the view of their banditti, as a sight 'See a tory woman' and striped her and her Children of all their Linen and Cloths." Peter Guire, of Connecticut, was branded on the forehead with the letters *G.R.* (George Rex). Samuel Jarvis, also of Connecticut, related that the following treatment made his whole family very ill:

That your Memorialist for his Attachment to constitutional Government was taken with his Wife and Famely, consisting of three Daughters and one little Son by a Mob of daring and unfeeling Rebels from his Dwelling House in the dead of Night Stripped of everything, put on board Whale Boats and Landed on Long Island in the Month of August last about 2 oClock in the Morning Oblieging them to wade almost to their Middle in the Water.

Probably the best-known mobbing in Philadelphia was that of Dr. John Kearsley, whose widow finally submitted a claim to the commissioners. Kearsley, a leading physician, pill manufacturer, and horse dealer, was a pugnacious American with strong Loyalist views. He was seized by a mob in September, 1775, and had his hand bayoneted; then he was carried through the streets to the tune of "Rogue's March." Sabine reports that he took off his wig with his injured hand and, "swinging it around his head, huzzaed louder and longer than his persecutors."

This display of spirit notwithstanding, he nearly died following this treatment, according to his widow. His house was later ransacked, he was arrested, and he finally died in jail.

Atrocious punishments of Loyalists were sometimes carried out by local authorities in semilegal fashion—it was noted that the tarring and feathering of a New York victim in 1775 "was conducted with that regularity and decorum that ought to be observed in all publick punishments." But just as often mobs, drumhead courts, and all the horrors of vigilante policing were found. Indeed it is possible that the term "lynch law" derives from Charles Lynch, a Bedford County, Virginia, justice of the peace who became renowned for his drastic, cruel action against neighboring Tories.

The number of Loyalists subjected to cruel, often extralegal, punishments can only be estimated, and likewise the number of those murdered or executed "legally" will never be known, but no one familiar with the sources— Whig newspapers are full of accounts of executions—can doubt that it is substantial, although the statement by a New York Loyalist that the rebels "made a practice of hanging people up on a slight pretence" is no doubt an exaggeration. Probably only fear of reprisals kept numbers from being much larger than they were. The carrying out of the supreme penalty was usually reserved for some overt aid to the British such as spying, piloting ships, guiding troops to the attack, recruiting, counterfeiting.

One of the most notorious executions of a Loyalist was that of John Roberts, a native-born Pennsylvania Quaker, who had aided the British occupying forces in Philadelphia and rather foolhardily had not departed with them. His trial was in 1778, and even many Whigs petitioned the authorities for a pardon, but in vain. A contemporary described the situation thus:

Roberts' wife, with ten children, went to Congress, threw themselves on their knees and supplicated mercy, but in vain. His behaviour at the gallows did honor to human nature. He told his audience that his conscience acquitted him of guilt; that he suffered for doing his duty to his Sovereign; that his blood would one day be demanded at their hands; and then turning to his children, charged and exhorted them to remember his principles, for which he died, and to adhere to them while they had breath. This is the substance of his speech; after which he suffered with the resolution of a Roman.

In 1792 the state of Pennsylvania restored Roberts' confiscated estate to his widow, Jane, a belated act of justice, for it seems Roberts had been a scapegoat, only one among so very many who had cooperated with the British. Roberts' behavior would doubtless have made him a remembered hero had he suffered for the other side. Similarly, in Connecticut, Moses Dunbar was tried and hanged for accepting a British commission and recruiting troops at about the same time that Nathan Hale suffered the same penalty. Connecticut honors Hale but forgets Dunbar. One of the more bizarre executions was reported by the *Boston Gazette* for November 3, 1777, under the date line Fishkill: "Last Thursday, one Taylor, a spy was hanged at Hurley, who was detected with a letter to Burgoyne, which he had swallowed in a silver ball, but the assistance of a tartar emetic he discharged the same."

But perhaps more moving across the years than accounts of atrocities are the more pedestrian misfortunes of war. Women in particular are always the great sufferers, being separated from their husbands and sons, living in constant dread of bereavement. In 1780 Mary Donnelly petitioned the British authorities in New York for relief. Her husband had been serving on board a privateer when "about seven months ago as my youngest Child lay expireing in my Arms an account came of the Vessil being lost in a Storm." Mrs. Donnelly was now destitute, "frequently being affraid to open my Eyes on the Daylight least I should hear my infant cry for Bread and not have it in my power to relieve him, the first meal I had eat for three days at one time was a morsel of dry bread and a lump of ice."

On June 6, 1783, Phebe Ward, of East Chester, wrote to her husband Edmund, a native of the province of New York:

Kind Husband

I am sorry to aquant you that our farme is sold . . . .

thay said if I did not quitt posesion that thay had aright to take any thing on the farme or in the house to pay the Cost of a law sute and imprisen me I have sufered most Every thing but death it self in your long absens pray Grant me spedy Releaf or God only knows what will be com of me and my frendsles Children

thay say my posesion was nothing youre husband has forfeted his estate by Joining the British Enemy with a free and vollentary will and thereby was forfeted to the State and sold

All at present from your cind and Loveing Wife                              phebe Ward

pray send me spedeay anser.

One of the most pathetic stories of all concerns Filer Dibblee, a native-born lawyer, and his family. In August, 1776, they fled from Stamford to Long Island, but a few months later the rebels turned Dibblee's wife and five children "naked into the Streets," having stolen the very clothes from their backs as well as having plundered the house. The family fled to New York City, where Dibblee obtained sufficient credit to settle at Oyster Bay, Long Island, but in 1778 the rebels plundered the family a second time and carried Dibblee as prisoner to Connecticut, where he remained imprisoned six months until exchanged. With further credit the family established themselves at Westhills, Long Island, where they were "plundered and stripped" a third time; then came a move to Hempstead, Long Island, and in 1780 a fourth ravaging. Dibblee now, for the first time, applied for relief from the commander in chief and received about one hundred dollars. In 1783 the whole family moved to St. John, New Brunswick, where they managed to survive a rough winter in a log cabin, but Dibblee's "fortitude gave way" at the prospect of imprisonment for his considerable indebtedness and the fate his family would suffer as a consequence. The result was that he "grew Melancholy, which soon deprived him of his Reason, and for months could not be left by himself," and finally in March, 1784, "whilst the Famely were at Tea, Mr Dibblee walked back and forth in the Room, seemingly much composed: but unobserved he took a Razor from the Closet, threw himself on the bed, drew the Curtains, and cut his own throat.

Shortly afterward the Dibblee house was accidentally burned to the ground, was then rebuilt by the heroic widow, only to be accidentally razed again the same year by an Indian servant girl.

It is not surprising that imprisonment and escape loom large in Loyalist annals. The most celebrated prison was in Connecticut at the Simsbury (now East Granby) copper mines, where the ruins still afford a dramatic prospect. The isolated and strongly Whig back country of Connecticut was considered a good spot to incarcerate important Loyalists from all over the Northern colonies, and the mines, converted into a prison in 1773, were ideal. The "Catacomb of Loyalty," to quote Thomas Anburey, or the "woeful mansion," to quote an inmate, contained cells forty-yards below the surface, into which "the prisoners are let down by a windlass into the dismal cavern, through a hole, which answers the purpose of conveying their food and air, as to light, it scarcely reaches them." The mere threat of the "Mines" could make a Loyalist conform. One prisoner regarded being sent there as a "Shocking Sentence (Worse than Death)." The mines received such celebrated Loyalists as Mayor Mathews of New York and William Franklin, who wrote of his "long and horrible confinement" and was described on his release as "considerably reduced in Flesh."

In May, 1781, there was a mass breakout. The leaders of the escape, Ebenezer Hathaway and Thomas Smith, arrived in New York some weeks later, and their alleged experiences were reported by Rivington's newspaper. Hathaway and Smith recalled that they had originally been captured on a privateer, sentenced, and marched the seventy-four miles from Hartford to Simsbury. The entrance to the dungeon was a heavily barred trap door that had to be raised

by means of a tackle, whilst the hinges grated as they turned upon their hooks, and opened the jaws and mouths of what they call Hell, into which they descended by means of a ladder about six feet more, which led to a large iron grate or hatchway, locked down over a shaft about three feet diameter, sunk through the solid rock. . . . They bid adieu to this world,

and went down thirty-eight feet more by ladder "when they came to what is called the landing; then marching shelf by shelf, till descending about thirty or forty feet more they came to a platform of boards laid under foot, with a few more put over head to carry off the water, which keeps continually dropping." There they lived for twenty nights with the other prisoners, using "pots of charcoal to dispel the foul air" through a ventilation hole bored from the surface until the opportunity to escape came when they were allowed up into the kitchen to prepare food and rushed and captured the guards.

Some colorful Connecticut escapes in other places are also recorded. Nathan Barnum avoided appearing for trial in 1780 by inoculating himself with smallpox, whereupon he was "sent to the Hospital, where he was chained to the Floor to prevent his Escape, he found Means to bribe one of the Nurses, who not only brought him a File to cut off his Irons, but amused the Centinal, placed over him while he effected it. . . ."

Samuel Jarvis and his brother got out of prison "by the assistance of Friends who had privately procured some Women's apparel which they Dressed themselves in, and by that means made their escape through the Rebel Army." James Robertson asserted that while he was in jail at Albany, the British attacked and set the building on fire, whereupon, unable to walk, he managed to crawl into a bed of cabbages "and chewing them to prevent being suffocated" was found three days later badly burnt.

There was even a series of Tory hiding places between New York and Canada, rather in the fashion of the "Underground Railroad" of the pre-Civil War days.

The treatment of imprisoned Loyalists ranged over the widest possible spectrum. Simsbury was notoriously the worst prison, almost the Andersonville of the time. Many Loyalists suffered close confinement in much pleasanter conditions; others merely underwent house arrest; others were only prevented from traveling; some were on parole and, if banished to some remote part of America, were boarded with reluctant Whigs. Some worked in the normal way by day and simply spent the night in jail. In 1776 Thomas Vernon, a fanatically early riser, was removed, with three other prominent Rhode Island Loyalists, from Newport to Glocester, in the northern part of the state, because he had refused the test oath. The foursome's journey and their few months' stay in Glocester were pleasant and gentlemanly, almost Pickwickian. The friends walked and admired the countryside, ate, drank, and conversed well in the local inn where they lived; they planted beans, killed snakes, trapped squirrels, fished, played Quadrille (a card game); they were very well treated by the ladies of the house and by neighboring females. Their chief complaints were the lack of books, some local abhorrence of Tories, particularly by the men (their landlord said "the town was very uneasy" at their being there), a few fleas, tedium from the lack of friends and family, and some stealing of their food by their far from genial host.

One Whig member of the Continental Congress opposed even the condemnation of a Loyalist pamphlet because it was "a strange freedom that was confined to one side of a question," but such enlightenment (or foolhardiness) was rare. Most active Whigs hated the Loyalists as "traitors." "I would have hanged my own brother had he taken part with our enemy in the contest," declared John Adams. It was a common observation that the Whigs held the Tories "in greater destestation" than the British, that their "inveteracy" was "inconceivable," and several Tory prisoners of the French attributed their harsh treatment to "misrepresentation" by the Whigs.

Benjamin Rush was so incensed by British mistreatment of his father that he resolved to "drive the first rascally Tory I meet with a hundred miles barefooted through the first deep snow falls in our country."

And, of course, greed and envy played a part. Crèvecoeur, through fictional characters, expressed valid motives for the Whig desire to attack the Tories. He has Aaron Blue-Skin, "a new-made squire," declare, "Oh, how it pleases me to bring the pride of these quondam gentry down! This is fulfilling the Bible to a tittle; this is lowering the high and rewarding the low; this is humbling the proud; this is exalting the Christian, the meek man." A lady Whig adds, " 'Tis best these rich fellows should go, for they won't fight, and by decamping they leave plaguy good fleeces behind."

Human suffering is always deplorable, but it is well to recall that the Whigs suffered from British and Tory persecution and would doubtless have suffered more if they had lost the war, as the harsh behavior of the one Loyalist legislature (in Georgia) that did meet during the war suggests.

In Britain Loyalist exiles encountered some anti-Americanism, but it was not serious or comparable to national Francophobia — no anti-Americanism was observed during the notorious Lord George Gordon riots of 1780. Although American property in Britain was not appropriated, the British, in fact, set some precedent for confiscation. As early as 1775 Parliament ordered the seizure of American ships and cargoes on the high seas; General Howe confiscated Whig property when he arrived in New York at the beginning of the war; in 1780 Governor Robertson shared out rebel lands among Loyalists in New York; and final victory might have meant an expropriation of American property reminiscent of that in conquered Ireland.

The Whigs suffered as the Tories did—legal persecution, mob action, imprisonment (the British prison ships were particularly horrible and gave rise to effective propagandist literature), and all the excesses of civil war. Adrian C. Leiby, the historian of the Hackensack Valley, for example, reports that there was barely a Whig family there that had not lost someone to a Tory raiding party. There is at least one recorded tarring and feathering of a Whig by British troops—of one Thomas Ditson, Jr., in Boston in March, 1775. In June, 1779, the *Virginia Gazette* reported the murder of a Whig captain by a party of Tories whom he had discovered robbing his house. A sentinel wounded him with a gunshot; then, after taking all the horses from the stable, the Tories pursued the captain into the house, where he was lying on a bed, and

immediately thrust their bayonets into his body several times, continuing the barbarity while they heard a groan; and lest life might still be remaining in him, they cut both his arms with a knife in the most inhuman manner. The villain who shot him, had been his neighbour and companion from his youth.

The victim lived another two days.

# Suggestions for Further Reading

The process of interpreting the American Revolution began with those who actually lived through the years of upheaval, rebellion, and nation-making. Particularly revealing are the studies of David Ramsay, *The History of the American Revolution* (2 vols., Philadelphia, 1789), and Mercy Otis Warren, *The History of the Rise, Progress and Termination of the American Revolution* (3 vols., Boston, 1805). While Ramsay and Warren represent many of their contemporaries who applauded American efforts in what they viewed as the noble struggle to protect human liberty, two loyalists, Thomas Hutchinson and Peter Oliver, were of a different mind. Hutchinson, the last royal governor of Massachusetts, did manage to maintain some detachment in the third volume of *The History of the Colony and Province of Massachusetts-Bay,* ed. Lawrence S. Mayo (Cambridge, 1936), which covers the years 1749–1774. But Peter Oliver, in his *Origin & Progress of the American Rebellion,* ed. Douglass Adair and John A. Schutz (San Marino, 1961), perceived the coming Revolution as the work of the devil in the guise of patriot leaders.

Loyalist writers have not had much influence on later interpretations. During the nineteenth century, for instance, the dominant mood held that the Revolution had revealed a united people in search of freedom from oppression. The establishment of liberty for all, seemingly as a part of God's "grand design," was the major theme in George Bancroft's *The History of the United States of America from the Discovery of the American Continent* (10 vols., Boston, 1834–1874).

Bancroft's grand design explanation has not had much influence on historians since his time. Early in the twentieth century a group commonly referred to as "conflict" historians especially questioned the people's initial involvement. Rather, they saw the Revolution developing in two-fold fashion, as described by Carl Lotus Becker in *The History of Political Parties in the Province of New York, 1760–1776* (Madison, 1909). Becker emphasized the opposition of unenfranchised and underprivileged inhabitants against local aristocrats in the provinces, rather than the general movement against Great Britain, and saw in the awakening masses the beginnings of a long-term drive toward democracy. Another conflict historian, Arthur Schlesinger, Sr., described the uneasiness felt by wealthy commercial interests toward the rising citizenry in *The Colonial Merchants and the American Revolution, 1763–1776,* (New York, 1917), while Charles A. Beard, in *An Economic Interpretation of the Constitution of the United States* (New York, 1913), portrayed the constitution-makers of 1787 as men with vested property interests to protect—interests that would be threatened by a newly-activated populace. To the conflict historians, then, the Founding Fathers were not the liberty-loving saints who had filled the pages of Bancroft and of John Fiske's *The Critical Period of American History, 1783–1789* (New York, 1888).

In the 1920s J. Franklin Jameson

brought many of the conflict school's themes together in *The American Revolution Considered as a Social Movement* (Princeton, 1926). Interpretations emphasizing formative internal conflict between the people and their traditional, but threatened, local leaders have been carried forward in the investigations of Merrill Jensen, *The Articles of Confederation: An Interpretation of the Social-Constitutional History of the American Revolution, 1774–1781* (Madison, 1940), and *The New Nation: A History of the United States during the Confederation, 1781–1789* (New York, 1950). Jensen later argued in "Democracy and the American Revolution," *Huntington Library Quarterly*, XX(1957), pp. 321–341, that the Revolution had inadvertently moved America in the direction of greater democracy, in spite of the fact that democracy was not an initial goal. Works in a similar vein include Elisha P. Douglass, *Rebels and Democrats: The Struggle for Equal Rights and Majority Rule during the American Revolution* (Chapel Hill, 1955), and Jensen's most recent book, *The American Revolution Within America* (New York, 1974).

After the Second World War, the focus of scholarly interpretation shifted again. The new mood was more conservative. Those writing in what has since been labeled the "consensus" school had more in common with historians like Bancroft, deemphasizing internal tensions and class conflict and stressing instead cooperation among the American people. See Clinton Rossiter's *Seedtime of the Republic* (New York, 1953), and Daniel J. Boorstin's *The Genius of American Politics* (Chicago, 1953). Rossiter took John Adams's "minds and hearts of the people" quotation literally, while Boorstin treated the people as moving pragmatically toward the recreation of uncorrupted British ideals and institutions in America. And in *The Liberal Tradition in America* (New York, 1955), Louis Hartz posited the goal as that of saving the world's freest society, a society untainted by Europe's feudal institutions.

In *Middle-Class Democracy and the Revolution in Massachusetts, 1691–1780* (Ithaca, 1955), Robert E. Brown sought to repudiate the conflict historians using themes later carried forward with B. Katherine Brown in *Virginia, 1705–1786: Democracy or Aristocracy?* (East Lansing, 1964). The Browns documented the presence of widespread voting rights among free white adult males in the colonies. Since individuals had to own property in order to qualify for the franchise, they concluded that middle-class freehold farmers were prevalent everywhere and united in the defense of democracy. Many of the ideas presented in the studies of the Browns, Rossiter, Boorstin, and Hartz have been synthesized in Edmund S. Morgan's *The Birth of the Republic, 1763–1789* (Chicago, 1956), and in Bernard Bailyn, "Political Experience and Enlightenment Ideals in Eighteenth-Century America," *American Historical Review*, LXVII (1962), pp. 339–351.

Bailyn's essay served as a transitional piece, pointing toward his subsequent full-scale analysis of the worldview propelling Americans into and through the Revolution. In his introduction to *Pamphlets of the American Revolution, 1750–1776*, Vol. I (Cambridge, 1965), later expanded and republished as *The Ideological Origins of the*

*American Revolution* (Cambridge, 1967), Bailyn looked at perceptions among united provincial Americans of a conspiracy to destroy their liberties. He has examined the antecedents of such thinking in British radical Whig writings and analyzed the colonists' acceptance of this opposition tradition in *The Origins of American Politics* (New York, 1968).

Aspects of English radical Whig thought as it affected the course of the Revolution have been studied by a number of historians, most notably Gordon S. Wood in *The Creation of the American Republic, 1776–1787* (Chapel Hill, 1969), which stresses more than Bailyn the period after the Declaration of Independence. Also of importance are Pauline Maier, *From Resistance to Revolution: Colonial Radicals and the Development of American Opposition to Britain, 1765–1776* (New York, 1972), and Richard D. Brown, *Revolutionary Politics in Massachusetts: The Boston Committee of Correspondence and the Towns, 1771–1774* (Cambridge, 1970). Maier explores crowd violence within the context of radical Whiggism; Brown looks at the Massachusetts Committee of Correspondence from the same angle. Jack P. Greene, however, in *The Quest for Power: The Lower Houses of Assembly in the Southern Royal Colonies, 1689–1776* (Chapel Hill, 1963), has not agreed with Bailyn and others over the relative importance of the opposition Whig tradition.

Recent scholars have attempted to move beyond the conflict and the consensus models of interpretation without necessarily accepting or rejecting the findings of either group. They have insisted that before final con-clusions are reached, the people of the Revolution—their goals, ideals, needs, expectations, and values—must be fully comprehended. The "New Left" school of thought resulted in a number of essays concentrating on specific groups of poorer people in early American society, as summarized in Jesse Lemisch, "The American Revolution Seen from the Bottom Up," in *Towards a New Past: Dissenting Essays in American History,* ed. Barton J. Bernstein (New York, 1967), pp. 4–29. A specific example of Lemisch's view is "Jack Tar in the Streets: Merchant Seamen in the Politics of Revolutionary America," *William and Mary Quarterly,* 3rd Sers., XXV (1968), pp. 371–407. Other New Left historians looked for colonial sources of radical protest against the established order, as in Staughton Lynd, *Class Conflict, Slavery, and the United States Constitution* (Indianapolis, 1967), and Bernard J. Friedman, "The Shaping of a Radical Consciousness in Provincial New York," *Journal of American History,* LVI (1970), pp. 781–801. These historians established the point that lumping the people of the Revolution together as one group could distort the reality of that event. In this vein students should also consult Eric Foner's *Tom Paine and Revolutionary America* (New York, 1976), and the collected essays in Alfred F. Young, ed., *The American Revolution: Explorations in the History of American Radicalism* (De Kalb, 1976).

A second recent scholarly trend has arisen from the efforts of social historians who have pored through non-traditional sources such as tax lists, wills, property deeds, and church and town records in an attempt to reconstruct the conditions of life facing the people of eighteenth-century America. Several of the resulting studies have concluded that property was becoming more unevenly distributed, leading to the creation of an elite which dominated social and political decision-making well before the Revolution. Jackson Turner Main's *The Social Structure of Revolutionary America* (Princeton, 1965), argues that the Revolution arrested the trend toward extremes in wealth and poverty. Data presented by Main in "Government by the People: The American Revolution and the Democratization of the Legislatures," *William and Mary Quarterly*, 3rd Sers., XXIII (1966), pp. 391–407, posited a major expansion in political opportunities for the people, especially in the holding of important political offices. Evidence that everyday citizens were moving into positions of power on the local levels of government even before 1776 appears in R. A. Ryerson, "Political Mobilization and the American Revolution: The Resistance Movement in Philadelphia, 1765 to 1776," *William and Mary Quarterly*, 3rd Sers., XXXI (1974), pp. 565–588.

Other historians have not been as sanguine about the Revolution's internal generation of new levels of social, political, or legal opportunities. In *Men in Rebellion: Higher Governmental Leaders and the Coming of the American Revolution* (New Brunswick, 1973), James Kirby Martin concluded that the transfer of power at the highest levels of government occurred within the political elite, a process from which the people eventually benefited, but not necessarily because Revolutionary leaders wanted it that way. Other recent investigations suggest that the people, especially the poor, failed to make gains from the Revolution. See James T. Lemon and Gary B. Nash, "The Distribution of Wealth in Eighteenth-Century America: A Century of Change in Chester County, Pennsylvania, 1693–1802," *Journal of Social History*, II (1968), pp. 1–24; Allan Kulikoff, "The Progress of Inequality in Revolutionary Boston," *William and Mary Quarterly*, 3rd Sers., XXVIII (1971), pp. 375–412; and Gary B. Nash, "Poverty and Poor Relief in Pre-Revolutionary Philadelphia," *William and Mary Quarterly*, 3rd Sers., XXXIII (1976), pp. 3–30. Also of value in this context is Ronald Hoffman, "The 'Disaffected' in the Revolutionary South," in *The American Revolution* ed. A. F. Young, pp. 275–316, and Kenneth A. Lockridge, "Social Change and the Meaning of the American Revolution," *Journal of Social History*, VI (1973), pp. 403–439. Linda Grant De Pauw's "Land of the Unfree: Legal Limitations on Liberty in Pre-Revolutionary America," *Maryland Historical Magazine* LXVIII (1973), pp. 355–368, argues that the Revolution fostered little in terms of legal or human rights. For a case study tracing the impact of the Revolution on the lives of one important, ostensibly homogeneous community, Concord, Massachusetts, see Robert A. Gross, *The Minutemen and Their World* (New York, 1976).

No general agreement has yet been reached in the analysis of the goals and motivations of the individuals who participated in mob activities during the late colonial and Revolutionary years. Earlier work, such as R. S. Longley's "Mob Activities in Revolutionary Massachusetts," *New England*

*Quarterly,* VI (1933), pp. 99-130, relied on the framework provided by the French social-psychologist Gustave Le Bon, as presented in *The Crowd: A Study of the Popular Mind* (London, 1909). Le Bon's mobs were mindless, irrational masses of people easily manipulated by willful, scheming incendiaries. This interpretation has lost almost all credibility among modern scholars of crowd behavior. Those who have more recently investigated mobs in the American Revolution have drawn heavily from George Rudé's *The Crowd in History, 1730-1848* (New York, 1964). Rudé's analysis of popular disturbances in England and France demonstrated that preindustrial crowds were purposeful in organization, discriminating in targets, and not overly destructive in their defense of group interests. Gordon S. Wood related the findings of Rudé to crowds in the American Revolution. In "A Note on Mobs in the American Revolution," *William and Mary Quarterly,* 3rd Sers., XXIII (1966), pp. 635-642, Wood suggested the possibility that American crowds viewed themselves as defending constitutional needs against arbitrary power. This theme has been developed more fully by Pauline Maier in "Popular Uprisings and Civil Authority in Eighteenth-Century America," *William and Mary Quarterly,* 3rd Sers., XXVII (1970), pp. 3-35, and *From Resistance to Revolution,* cited above.

Maier stated that crowds were broad-based collections of all types of people in provincial communities, a position which has been challenged by Jesse Lemisch's "Jack Tar in the Streets," cited above. Others who disagree with Wood and Maier are Edward Country-man, "The Problem of the Early American Crowd," *Journal of American Studies,* VII (1973), pp. 77-90; Gary B. Nash, "Social Change and the Growth of Prerevolutionary Urban Radicalism," in *The American Revolution,* ed. A. F. Young, pp. 5-36; and Dirk Hoerder, "Boston Leaders and Boston Crowds, 1765-1776, "in *ibid.,* pp. 235-271. Nash's essay focuses on economic distress among the poor as a motivating factor for violence, while Hoerder studies the traditions that helped bring working people together in violent protest. See also E. P. Thompson, "The Moral Economy of the English Crowd in the Eighteenth Century," *Past & Present,* L (1971), pp. 76-136, and Richard Maxwell Brown, *Strain of Violence: Historical Studies of American Violence and Vigilantism* (New York, 1975).

A number of valuable monographs have appeared over the years dealing with specific Revolutionary individuals, groups, and events which relate to incidents of violence. Students should consider the following sample of studies in examining who participated in crowd actions and why: Irving Mark, *Agrarian Conflicts in Colonial New York* (New York, 1940); Richard Walsh, *Charleston's Sons of Liberty* (Columbia, 1959); Edmund S. and Helen M. Morgan, *The Stamp Act Crisis: Prologue to Revolution* (rev. ed., New York, 1962); Benjamin Woods Labaree, *The Boston Tea Party* (New York, 1964); Hiller B. Zobel, *The Boston Massacre* (New York, 1970); Patricia U. Bonomi, *A Factious People: Politics and Society in Colonial New York* (New York, 1971); Charles S. Olton, *Artisans for Independence: Philadelphia Mechanics and the Amer-*

*ican Revolution* (Syracuse, 1975), and Roger J. Champagne, *Alexander Mc-Dougall and the American Revolution in New York* (Syracuse, 1975).

Studies on blacks in bondage in Revolutionary America have been as contradictory as those on the nature, composition, and goals of the crowds. A general introduction is Benjamin Quarles, *The Negro in the American Revolution* (Chapel Hill, 1961), which stresses gains made through the Revolution. Differing in tone from Quarles is the quasi-Marxist analysis of Herbert Aptheker, *The Negro in the American Revolution* (New York, 1940). John Hope Franklin presents a factual overview in *From Slavery to Freedom: A History of Negro Americans* (3rd ed., New York, 1967), pp. 126–165. A masterful recent work not confined to the North American experience but taking a comparative approach is David Brion Davis, *The Problem of Slavery in the Age of Revolution, 1770–1823* (Ithaca, 1975). Davis's synthesis also analyzes emerging antislavery challenges to the "peculiar institution" in the western world.

The most thorough treatment of evolving white perceptions of blacks during the colonial and Revolutionary periods appears in Winthrop D. Jordan, *White Over Black: American Attitudes Toward the Negro, 1550–1812* (Chapel Hill, 1968). Jordan and Duncan J. MacLeod, *Slavery, Race, and the American Revolution* (New York, 1974), suggest that the Revolution had the potential to overwhelm chattel slavery in North America, but many other scholars disagree, among them David Brion Davis, Robert McColley, *Slavery and Jeffersonian Virginia* (Urbana, 1964), Donald L. Robinson, *Slavery*

*in the Structure of American Politics, 1765–1820* (New York, 1971), and Gerald W. Mullin, *Flight and Rebellion: Slave Resistance in Eighteenth-Century Virginia* (New York, 1972). The latter position received support from the controversial quantitative investigations of Robert W. Fogel and Stanley L. Engerman, *Time on the Cross: The Economics of American Negro Slavery* (2 vols., Boston, 1974). Fredrika T. Schmidt and Barbara R. Wilhelm, "Early Proslavery Petitions in Virginia," *William and Mary Quarterly,* 3rd Sers., XXX (1973), pp. 133–146, demonstrate that many Virginians remained deeply committed to slavery during the Revolution, even to the point of protesting a 1782 state law permitting private acts of manumission.

Another area of scholarly focus has been the examination of the words and deeds of the Founding Fathers relative to slavery. The debate has primarily concerned Thomas Jefferson. Agreeing with Winthrop D. Jordan, cited above, that Jefferson held deep-seated racial prejudices which undercut his push for total emancipation is William Cohen, "Thomas Jefferson and the Problem of Slavery," *Journal of American History,* LVI (1969), pp. 503–526. William W. Freehling, in "The Founding Fathers and Slavery," *American Historical Review,* LXXVII (1972), pp. 81–93, provides the dissenting voice. Freehling argues that the Founding Fathers attacked slavery where they could, for instance, by cutting off the importations of Africans. They hoped that time and circumstances would result in other means of dislodging the peculiar institution. In this context, Fawn M. Brodie's

*Thomas Jefferson: An Intimate History* (New York, 1974), takes a debunking psychohistorical look at the Virginia planter, especially of his reputed liaison with slave Sally Hemings. Edmund S. Morgan, in *American Slavery—American Freedom: The Ordeal of Colonial Virginia* (New York, 1975), transcends these particulars to search for a resolution to the paradox of how slavery and freedom developed simultaneously in the American colonies.

The roots of American abolitionism normally are associated with the Revolution and Quakers, who were quite active in speaking out against human bondage. Students should consult Sydney V. James, *A People Among Peoples: Quaker Benevolence in Eighteenth-Century America* (Cambridge, 1963), and Richard Bauman, *For the Reputation of Truth: Politics, Religion, and Conflict Among the Pennsylvania Quakers, 1750–1800* (Baltimore, 1971), for aspects of Quaker abolitionism. Gary B. Nash, in "Slaves and Slaveowners in Colonial Philadelphia," *William and Mary Quarterly,* 3rd Sers., XXX (1973), pp. 223-256, points out that Quaker benevolence was not necessarily selfless or all-pervasive—the movement against slavery coincided with new supplies of white indentured laborers in prerevolutionary Philadelphia.

Until recently, the interpretive literature on American women during the Revolutionary era has been more limited in quantity than that on chattel slaves. During the nineteenth and early twentieth centuries those who wrote about provincial women cast their subjects in genteel, "ladylike" molds. Typical is the detailed series by Elizabeth F. Ellet, *The Women of*

the American Revolution (3 vols., New York, 1853-1854), Other examples include Elizabeth Anthony Dexter, *Colonial Women of Affairs* (2nd ed., Boston, 1931); Elizabeth Cometti, "Women in the American Revolution," *New England Quarterly,* XX (1947), pp. 329-346; Walter Hart Blumenthal, *Women Camp Followers of the American Revolution* (Philadelphia, 1965); and Sally Smith Booth, *The Women of '76* (New York, 1973).

Despite these investigations of gentility, a few studies besides John Todd White's, included in this volume, have appeared which find this tradition fallacious in getting at the role of women in the Revolution. Two earlier exceptions which were more probing in conceptualization than volumes in the Ellet tradition are Mary Sumner Benson, *Women in Eighteenth-Century America: A Study of Opinion and Social Usage* (New York, 1935), and Julia C. Spruill, *Women's Life and Work in the Southern Colonies* (Chapel Hill, 1938). The notion that women, especially widows, were more free to develop themselves fully as individuals before the Revolution gained some credence from such works, but that generalization has not held up well in recent years. See, for instance, the valuable investigations of Carol R. Berkin, *Within the Conjurer's Circle: Women in Colonial America* (Morristown, 1974); the first three chapters of Mary P. Ryan, *Womanhood in America: From Colonial Times to the Present* (New York, 1975); Alexander Keyssar, "Widowhood in Eighteenth-Century Massachusetts: A Problem in the History of the Family," *Perspectives in American History,* VIII (1974), pp. 83-119; and Joan Hoff Wilson,

"The Illusion of Change: Women and the American Revolution," in *The American Revolution,* ed. A. F. Young, pp. 385-445. In these studies the changing status of women has been explained more as a function of social, demographic, and familial patterns in precapitalist America than in terms of factors related to the American Revolution.

The role of American women in the Revolution by comparison has been related to the concept of "republican motherhood," as discussed by Linda Kerber in "Daughters of Columbia: Educating Women for the Republic, 1787-1805," in *The Hofstadter Aegis: A Memorial,* ed. Stanley Elkins and Eric McKitrick (New York, 1974), pp. 36-59. Mary Beth Norton, in "Eighteenth-Century American Women in Peace and War: The Case of the Loyalists," *William and Mary Quarterly,* 3rd Sers., XXXIII (1976), pp. 386-409, presents another angle from this interpretive point of view.

As in the case of women, it has been a painstaking scholarly task to rescue the loyalists from the miasma of mythology about Revolutionary America. Until well into the nineteenth century, no one seemed to want to study the loyalists. But Lorenzo Sabine challenged patriotic convention in preparing his *Biographical Sketches of Loyalists of the American Revolution* (2 vols., Boston, 1864). His introductory essay confirmed the impression that loyalists were largely well-placed conservatives with an essential stake in a British-controlled America, a theme carried forward in Moses Coit Tyler, "The Party of the Loyalists in the American Revolution," *American Historical Review,* I (1895), pp. 24-45;

Claude H. Van Tyne, *The Loyalists in the American Revolution* (New York, 1902); and Leonard W. Labaree, "The Nature of American Loyalism," *Proceedings* of the American Antiquarian Society, LIV (1944), pp. 15-58.

Beginning in the 1960s, a number of studies began to move beyond the proposition that loyalists were advantaged standpatters. William H. Nelson's *The American Tory* (New York, 1961), remains the standard summary portraying the loyalists as ineffectively organized "cultural minorities." In *The King's Friends: The Composition and Motives of American Loyalist Claimants* (Providence, 1965), Wallace Brown draws upon the records of the British Loyalists' Claims Commission to demonstrate that tories were not just from the ranks of the wealthy. Brown's findings, as well as those of Mary Beth Norton, cited above, should be read in conjunction with Eugene R. Fingerhut, "Uses and Abuses of the Loyalists' Claims: A Critique of Quantitative Analysis," *William and Mary Quarterly,* 3rd Sers., XXV (1968), pp. 245-258. Brown broadened the meaning of his findings from the Claims records in *The Good Americans: The Loyalists in the American Revolution* (New York, 1969). His conclusions concerning the treatment of loyalists should be compared with those of Robert R. Palmer, *The Age of the Democratic Revolution, 1760-1820: The Challenge* (Princeton, 1959), pp. 185-206, in which Palmer claims that the severe treatment meted out to loyalists may be a measure of the Revolution's radicalizing force, at least in terms of handing authority to the people.

Much of the work on loyalist ideology has developed as an indirect result of Bailyn's *Ideological Origins of the American Revolution.* A good starting point is William A. Benton's *Whig-Loyalism: An Aspect of Political Ideology in the American Revolutionary Era* (Rutherford, 1969); Mary Beth Norton's *The British-Americans: The Loyalist Exiles in England, 1774–1789* (Boston, 1972); James Kirby Martin's "The Rights of Man and the American Revolution: Samuel Adams, Thomas Hutchinson, and John Dickinson," in *Men, Women, and Issues in American History,* ed. Howard Quint and Milton Cantor (Homewood, 1975), pp. 63–83; Bernard Bailyn's *The Ordeal of Thomas Hutchinson* (Cambridge, 1974); and Robert McCluer Calhoon's *The Loyalists in Revolutionary America, 1760–1781* (New York, 1973).

No supplementary listing of suggested readings can do full justice to the richness and variety of the writings on the American Revolution. Guides to other sources should be consulted, including John Shy, comp., *The American Revolution* (Chicago, 1973), and the appropriate sections of Frank Freidel *et al.,* eds., *The Harvard Guide to American History* (rev. ed., 2 vols., Cambridge, 1974).